Hamilton Ontario Book 1 in Colour Photos, Saving Our History One Photo at a Time

Photography
by Barbara Raué
2014

Series Name:
Cruising Ontario

Book 87 – Hamilton Book 1

Cover photo: Dundurn Castle

Series Name: Cruising Ontario
Saving Our History One Photo at a Time
in colour photos

Other Books by Barbara Raue

Coins of Gold

Arrows, Indians and Love

The Life and Times of Barbara
Volume 1: Inventions That Have Enhanced My Life
Volume 2: Entertainment That I Have Enjoyed
Volume 3: East Coast Trips
Volume 4: Olympics Have Always Intrigued Me
Volume 5: Wonders of the World
Volume 6: Caribbean Cruises We Have Enjoyed
Volume 7: Animals
Volume 8: Storms and Other Major Disasters in My Lifetime
Volume 9: Wars, Terrorist Attacks and Major Disasters

The Cromwell Family Book

Laura Secord Discovered

Visit Barbara's website to view all of her books
http://barbararaue.ca

John Ryckman, born in Barton township (where present day downtown Hamilton is), described the area in 1803 as he remembered it: The city in 1803 was all forest. The shores of the bay were difficult to reach or see because they were hidden by a thick, almost impenetrable mass of trees and undergrowth... Bears ate pigs, so settlers warred on bears. Wolves gobbled sheep and geese, so they hunted and trapped wolves. They also held organized raids on rattlesnakes on the mountainside. There was plenty of game. Many a time have I seen a deer jump the fence into my back yard, and there were millions of pigeons which we clubbed as they flew low."

Hamilton, the centre of a densely populated and industrialized region, is located in Southern Ontario on the western part of Lake Ontario. Hamilton Harbour marks the northern limit of the city, and the Niagara Escarpment runs through the middle of the city bisecting it into "upper" and "lower" parts. There are over one hundred waterfalls and cascades within the city, most of which are on or near the Bruce Trail as it winds through the Niagara Escarpment.

Two steel manufacturing companies, Stelco and Dofasco, were formed in 1910 and 1912, and Procter & Gamble opened a manufacturing plant in 1914. McMaster University moved from Toronto to Hamilton, an airport was built in 1940, a Studebaker assembly line started in 1948, the Burlington Bay Skyway Bridge was built in 1958, and the first Tim Horton's store opened in 1964.

On January 1, 2001, the new City of Hamilton was formed through the amalgamation of the former city and the six municipalities of Stoney Creek, Glanbrook, Ancaster, Dundas, and Flamborough. We have lived in Hamilton for more than 40 years; it is here that we raised our three children.

Table of Contents

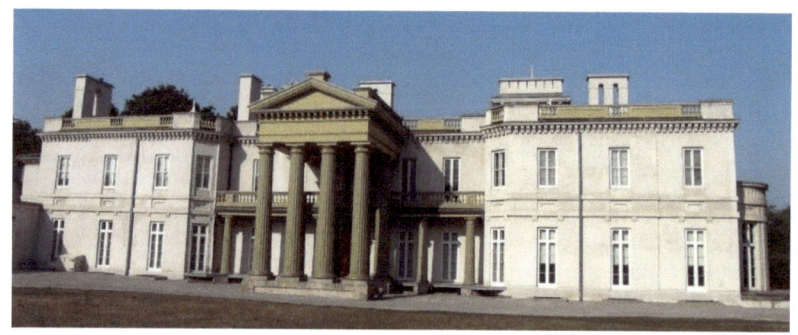

Dundurn Castle – pediment above two-storey pillars, cornice brackets, second floor balcony

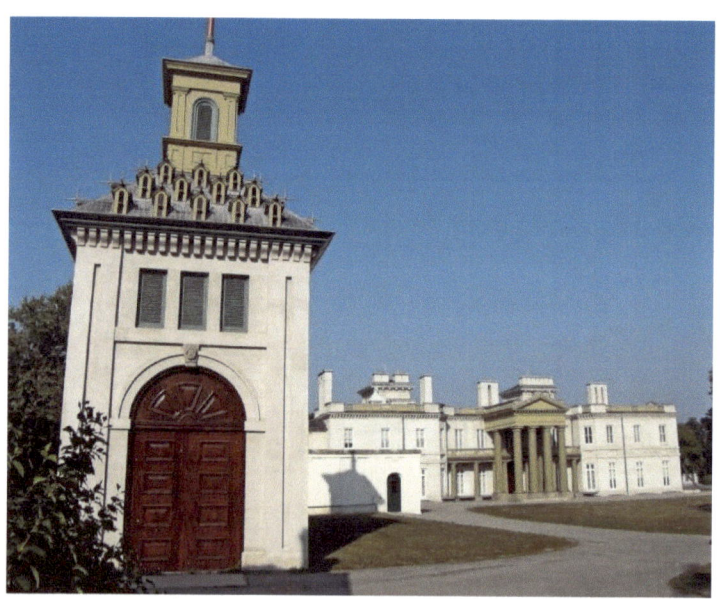

Dundurn Castle – completed in 1835 for Allan Napier MacNab; cupola

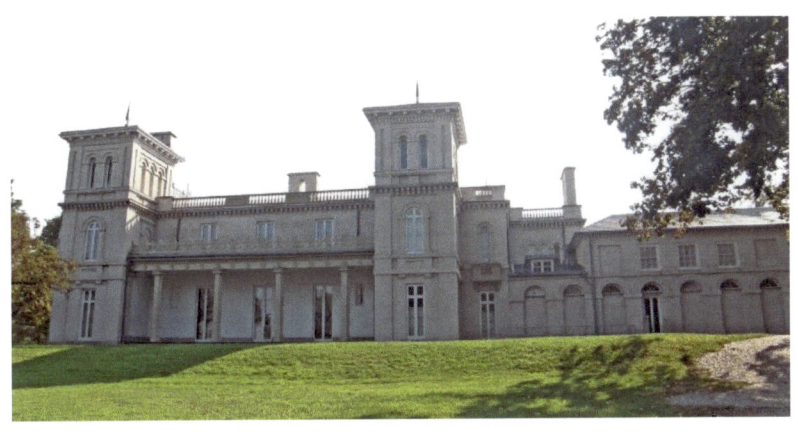

Dundurn Castle from the rear
Classical and Italianate styles; three-storey towers,
French windows, broad balconies
View of Burlington Bay

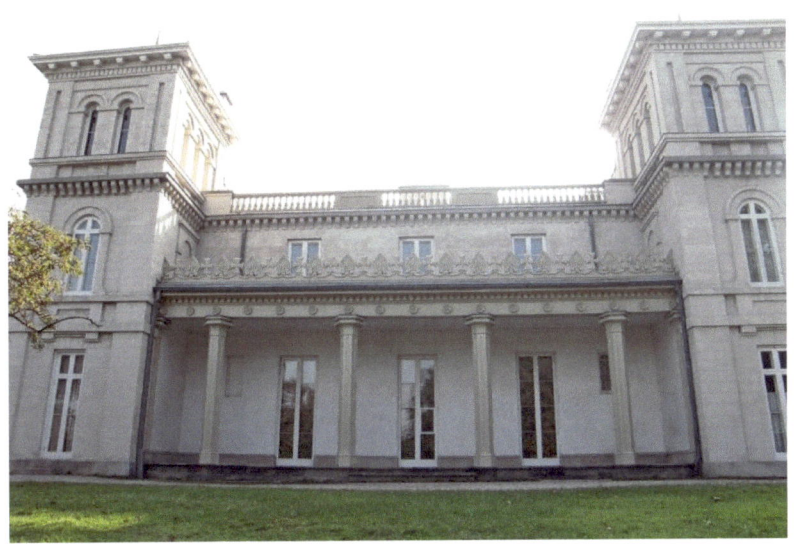

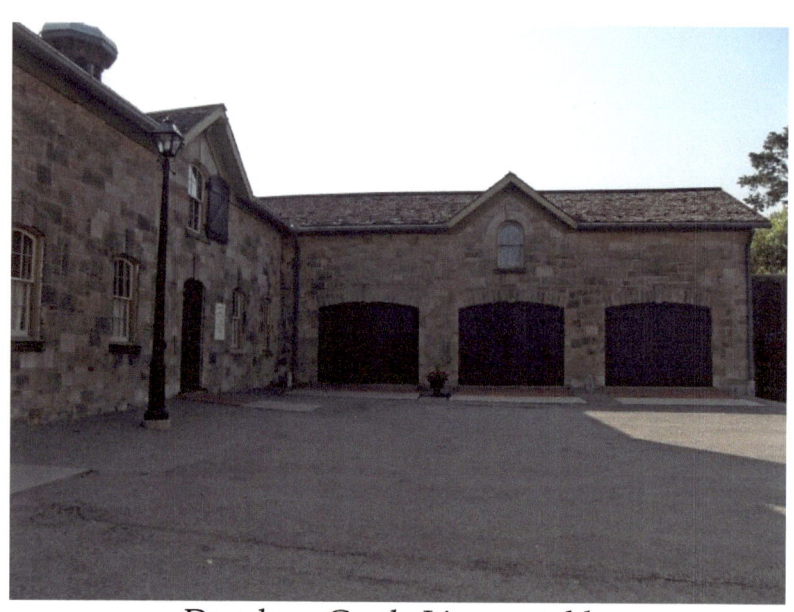

Dundurn Castle Livery stable

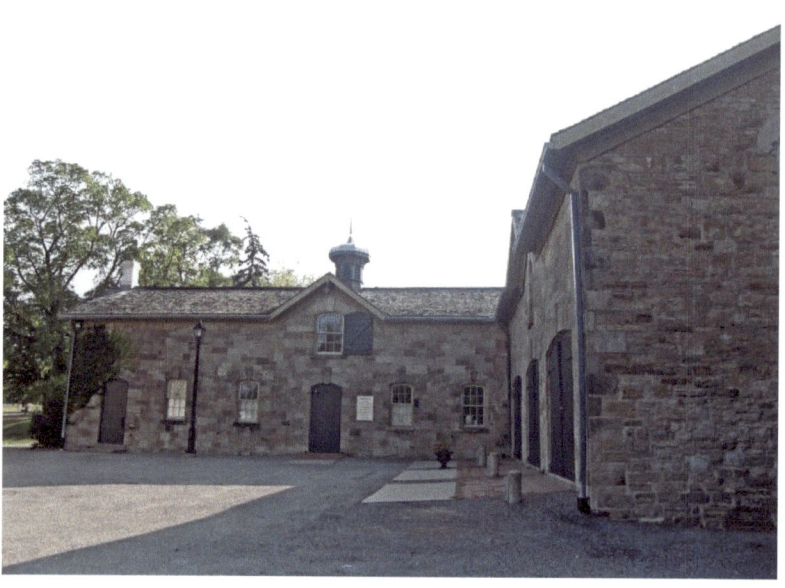

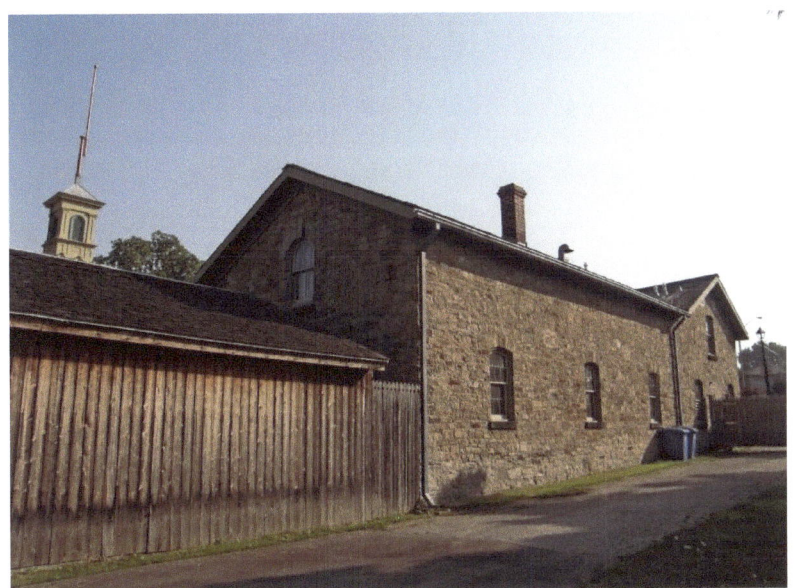

Rear of livery stable

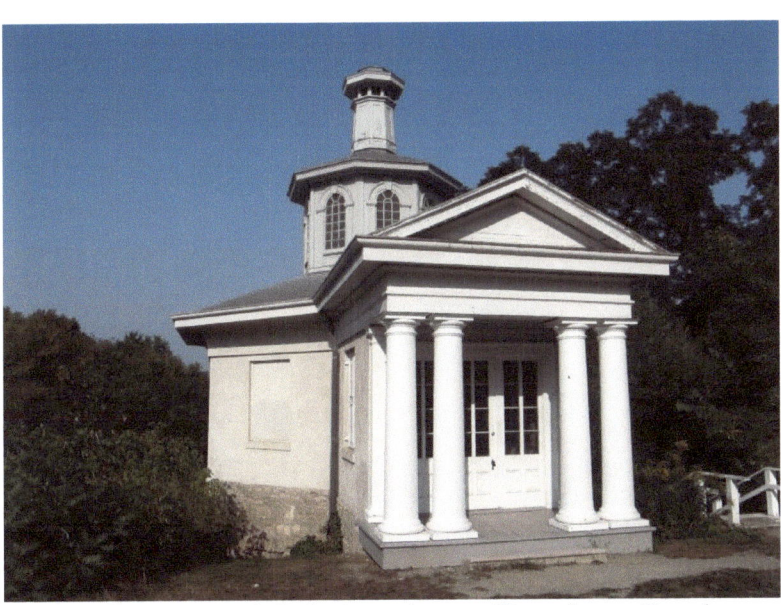

Perhaps a cockfighting ring at Dundurn Castle

Charlton Avenue

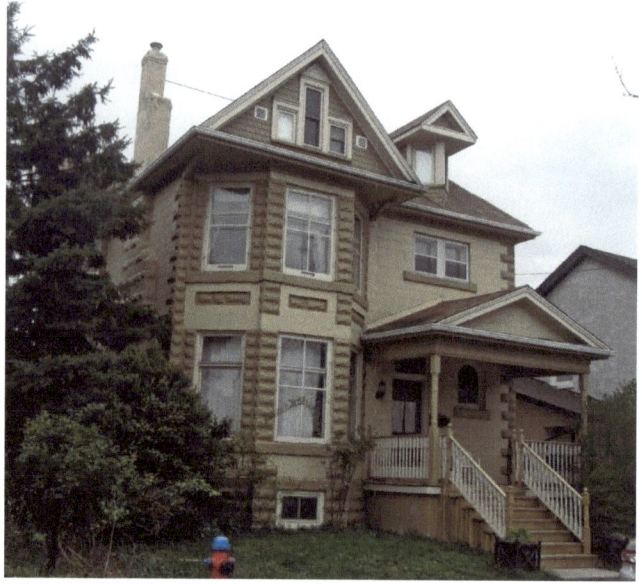

Edwardian – Palladian window, two-storey bay window, dormer in attic

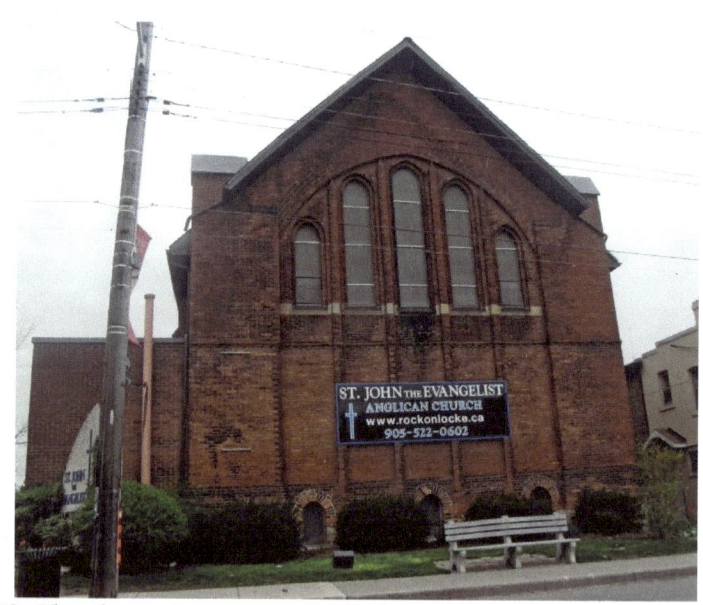

320 Charlton Avenue - St. John the Evangelist Church

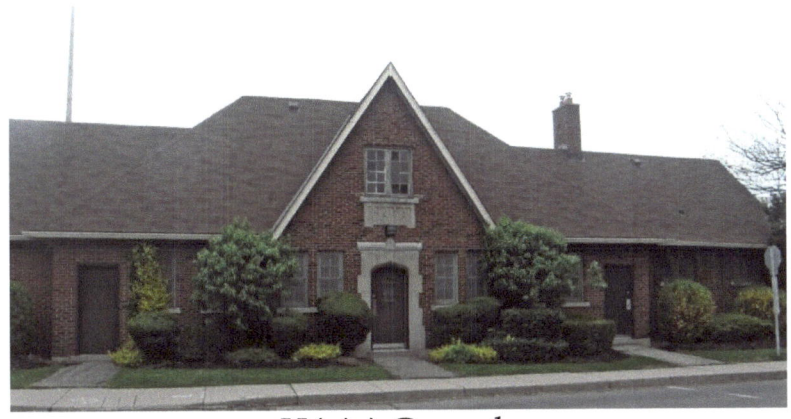

HAAA Grounds
Charlton Avenue West between Locke and Queen Streets

The original 1874 plans for the six-and-one-half-acre site, owned by the Hamilton Cricket Club, included an eight foot board fence, a dining room, dressing room, and grandstand. In addition to cricket, lacrosse and rugby football were played here. Immediately to the north was one of Hamilton's earliest steeplechase courses. In 1910, the Tiger Rugby Club amalgamated with the cricket club which led to the formation of the Hamilton Amateur Athletic Association (H.A.A.A.). By October 1910 a new steel grandstand which seated 2,318 had been constructed on the west side of the field. The Grey Cup Game was played here in October of that year. The grandstand, destroyed by fire on September 27, 1927, was rebuilt. In 1945, the City of Hamilton purchased the H.A.A.A. grounds. The Hamilton Tigers played here until 1950, after which high school and junior football teams took over the facility. The H.A.A.A. Grounds is the oldest sports park in Hamilton.

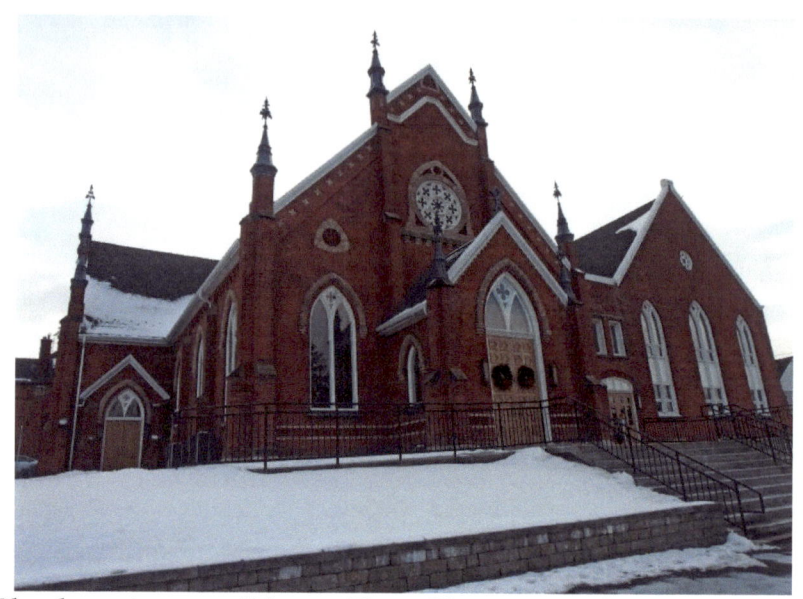

Charlton Avenue West – First Christian Reformed Church buttresses

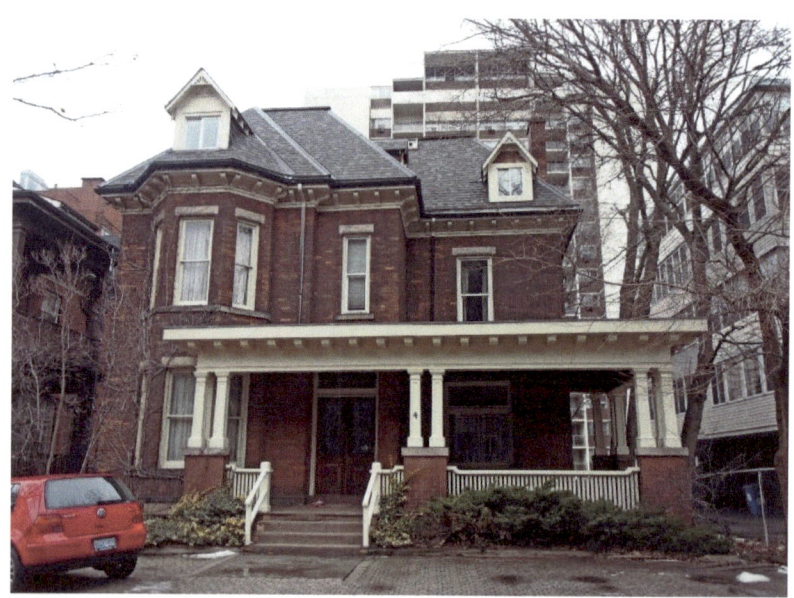

44 Charlton Avenue West – dormers, two-storey bay window, cornice backets

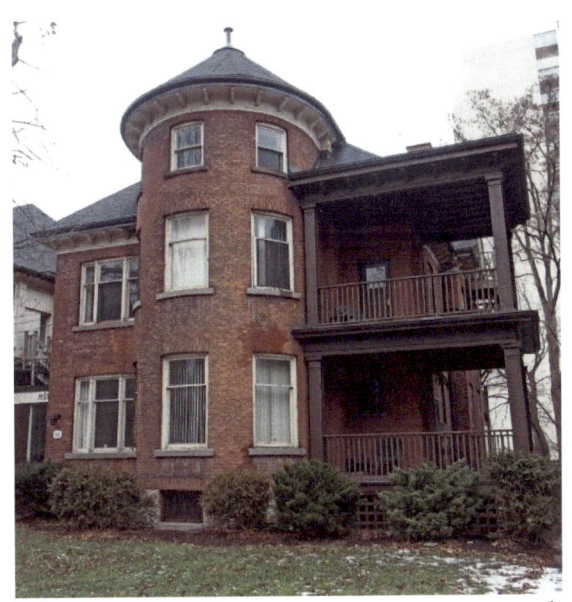

52 Charlton Avenue West – Queen Anne style, turret

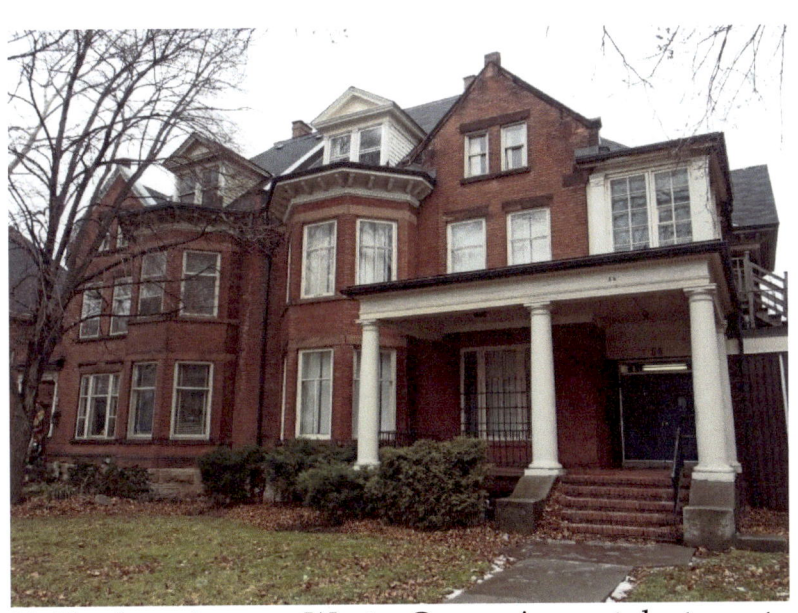

56-64 Charlton Avenue West – Queen Anne style, two-storey bay windows, dormers

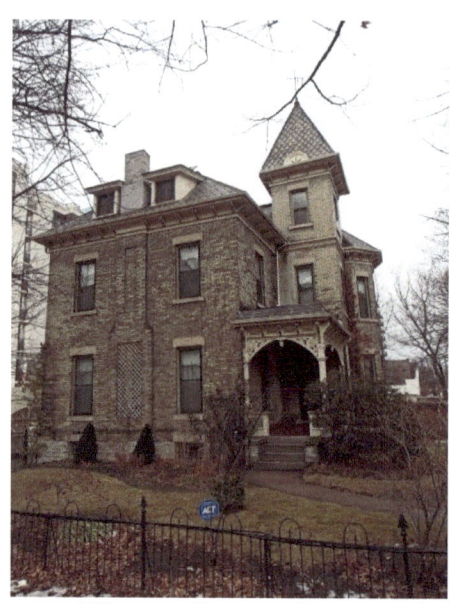

72 Charlton Avenue West – Queen Anne style, turret, dormers

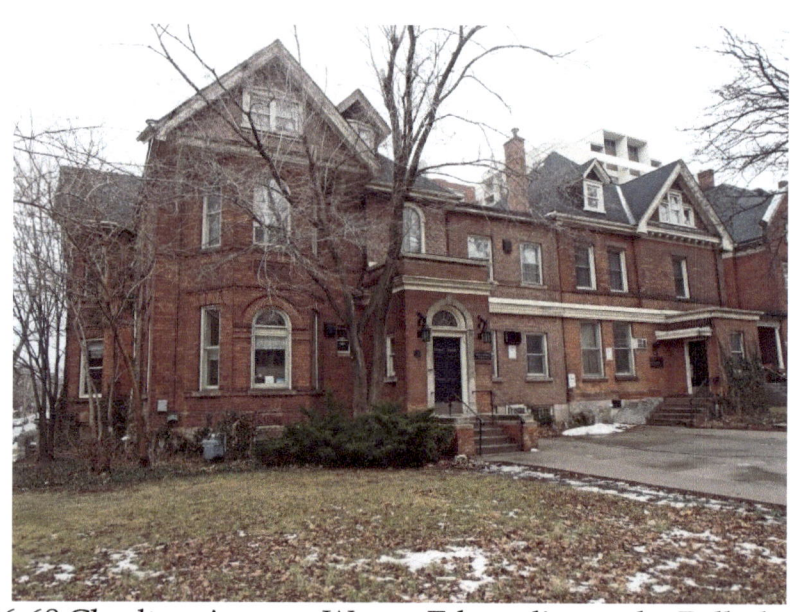

66-68 Charlton Avenue West – Edwardian style, Palladian window, arched window voussoirs

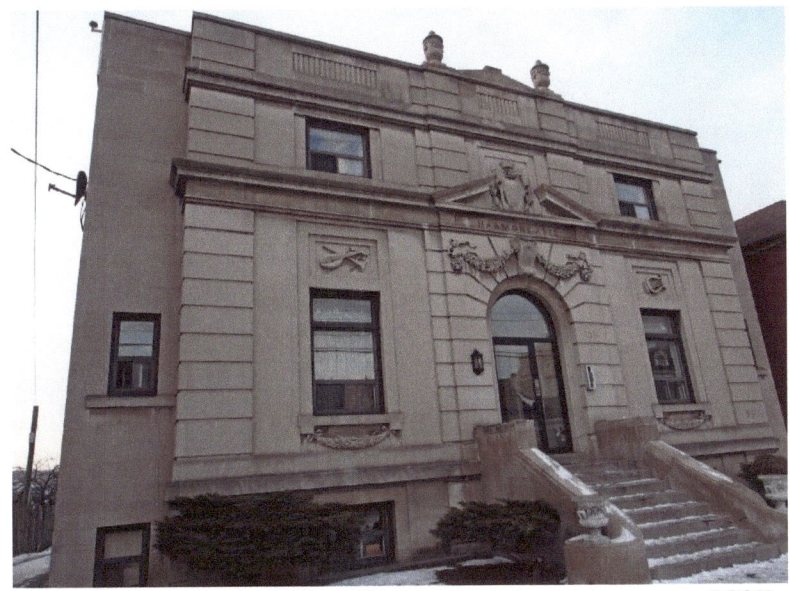

245 Bay Street North – Harmony Apartments – 1935

Dr. Vincenzo Agro was born in Sicily where he studied medicine. In the early 1920s fascism began to take root in Italy and he was not comfortable with it. Doc left his homeland and came to Hamilton to set up his practice in 1926. He built this hall where Italians new to this country could gather for dances, plays, pageants, and concerts. The Hall, called "La Sala" was built in 1935.

In June 1940, Italian leader Benito Mussolini declared war on the Allies. Hamilton's Italians immediately became the enemy. Dozens of tailors, grocers, musicians, and steelworkers were rounded up and sent to the Petawawa internment camp.

As a result, La Sala became Harmony Apartments.

Doc continued to practice and died in 1965.

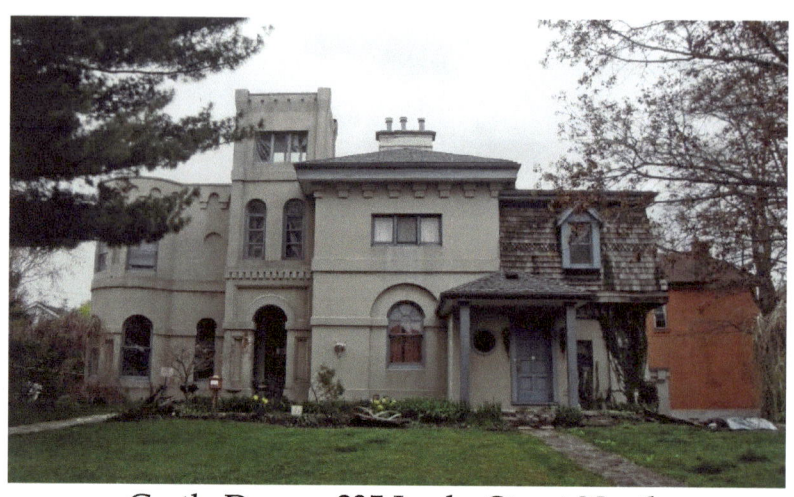

Castle Doune, 235 Locke Street North

Sir Allan MacNab hired Robert Wetherell to design his Regency residence between 1835 and 1840. Castle Doune, once called St. Mary's Lodge, was a Gate Lodge for the superintendent of Dundurn. The house was enlarged in 1908 with the turret and rounded bay on the southern half. The chimney and windows are features of Dundurn Castle.

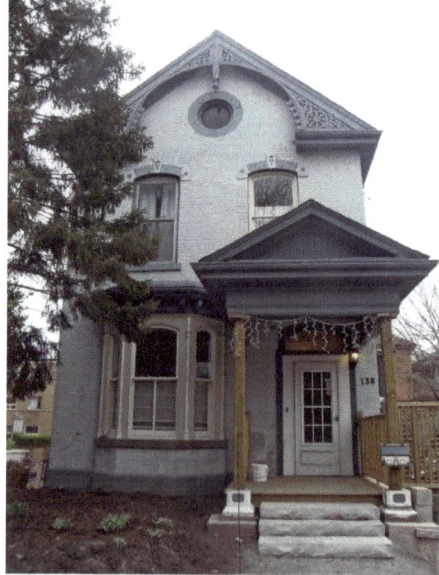

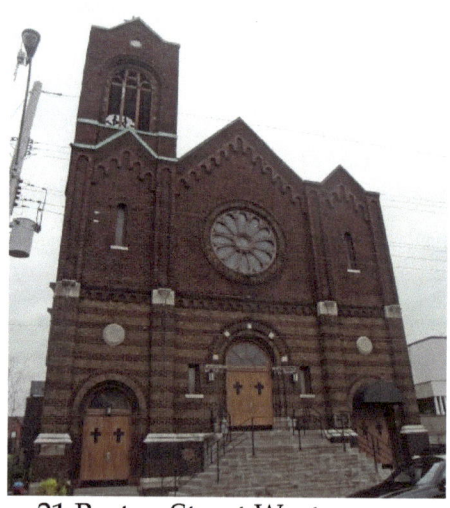

138 James Street North
Gothic Revival, pediment,
verge board trim on gable & finial

21 Barton Street West
All Souls Church – A.D.1922
rose window, corbelled dentils

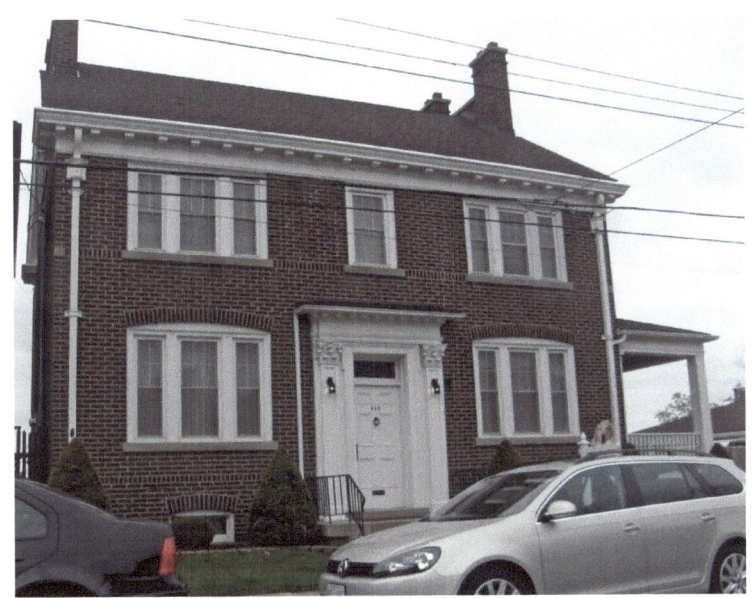

#439 Bay Street North

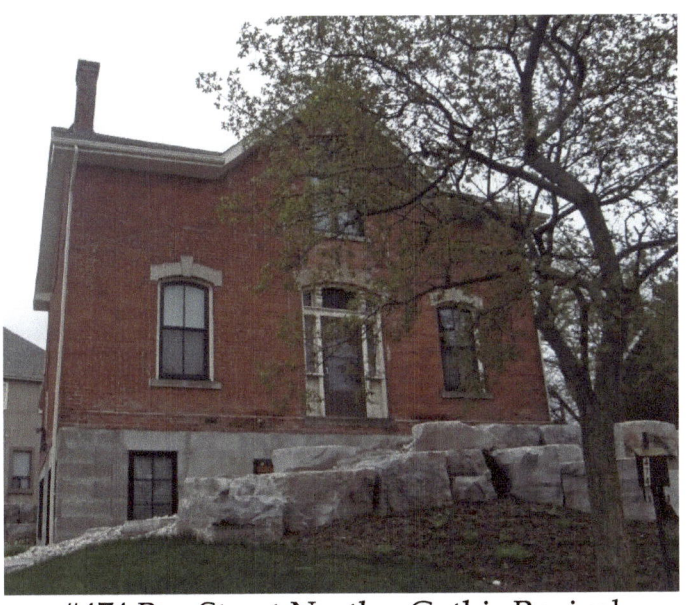

#474 Bay Street North – Gothic Revival

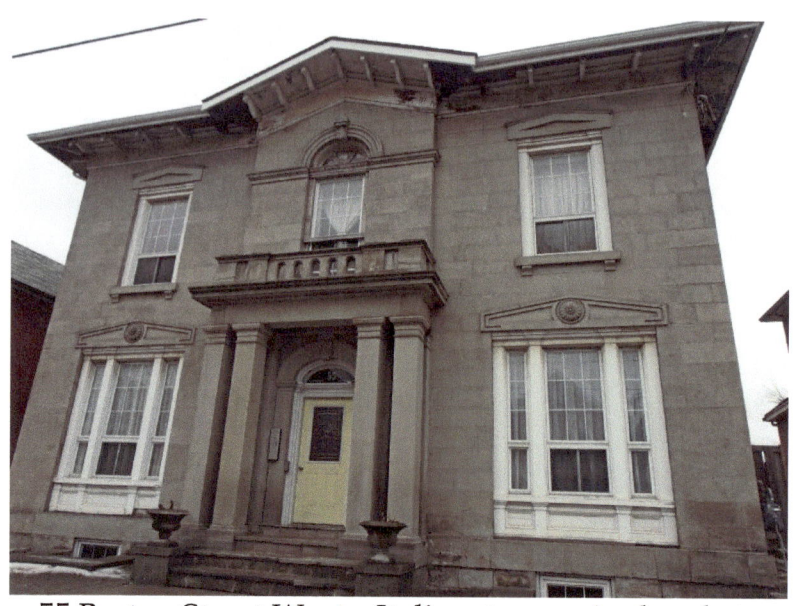

55 Barton Street West – Italianate, cornice brackets
Balcony above pillared entrance

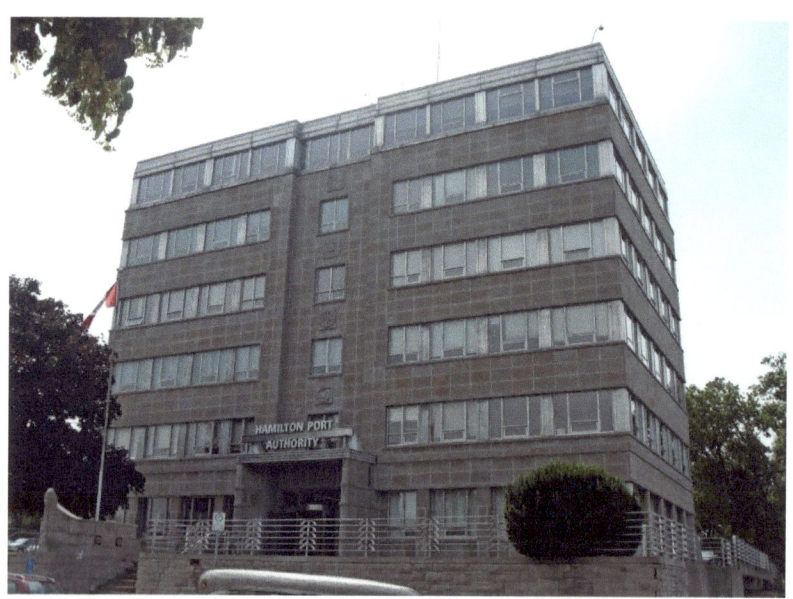

Hamilton Port Authority on James Street North

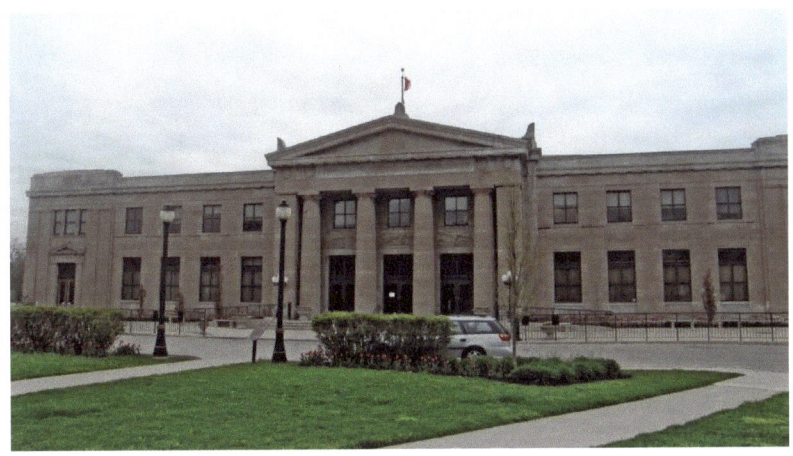

Canadian National Railway Station, 360 James Street North built in 1931Neo-classical style. The first passenger train left the station on February 20, 1930. The station was closed in 1993. In 1996, Hollywood producers of the movie "The Long Kiss Goodbye" offered CN $1 million to renovate the station and shoot part of the movie there. The publicity from this attracted the Labourer's International Union of North America (LIUNA) who bought the station and spent $3 million in renovations to open it as a hall for weddings and other events.

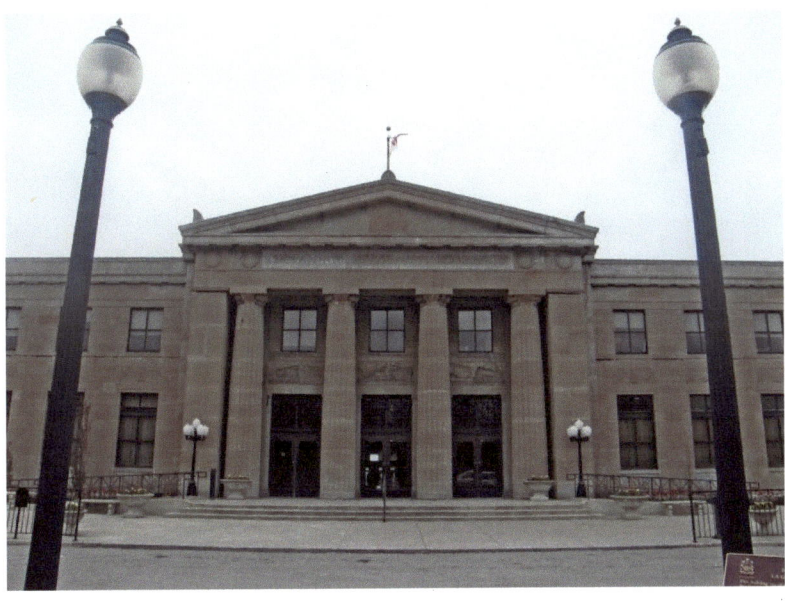

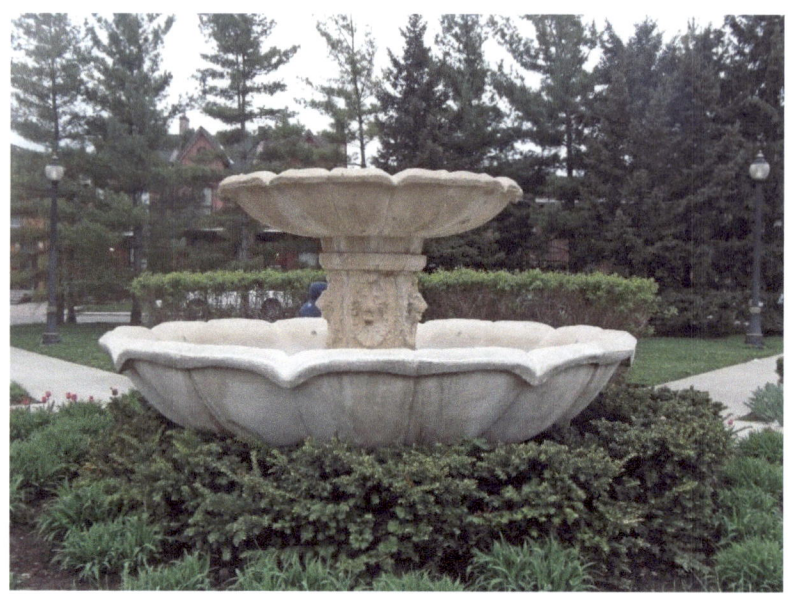

Fountain located in the park to the south of the CN Station

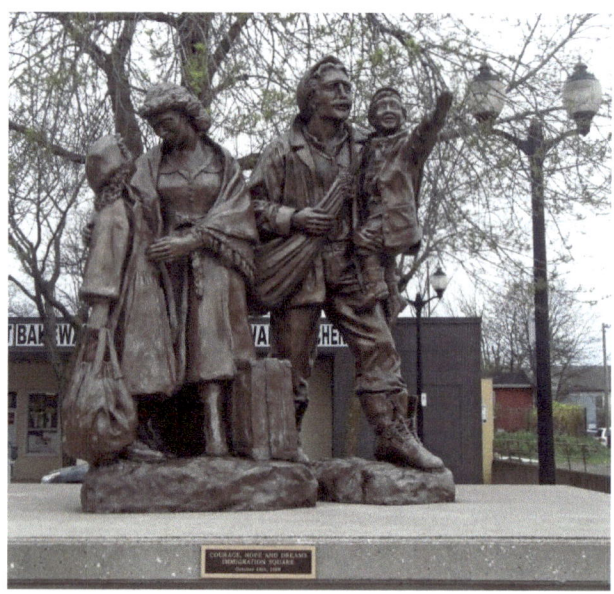

Courage, Hope and Dreams - Immigration Square
October 14, 2000

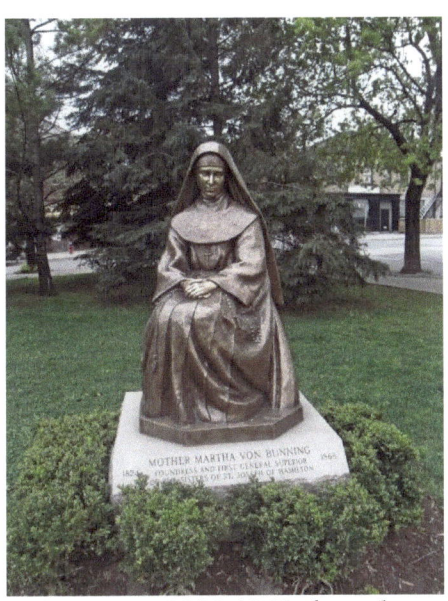

Mother Martha von Bunning 1824-1868, foundress and First General
Superior of the Sisters of St. Joseph of Hamilton located in the park
to the south of the CN Station

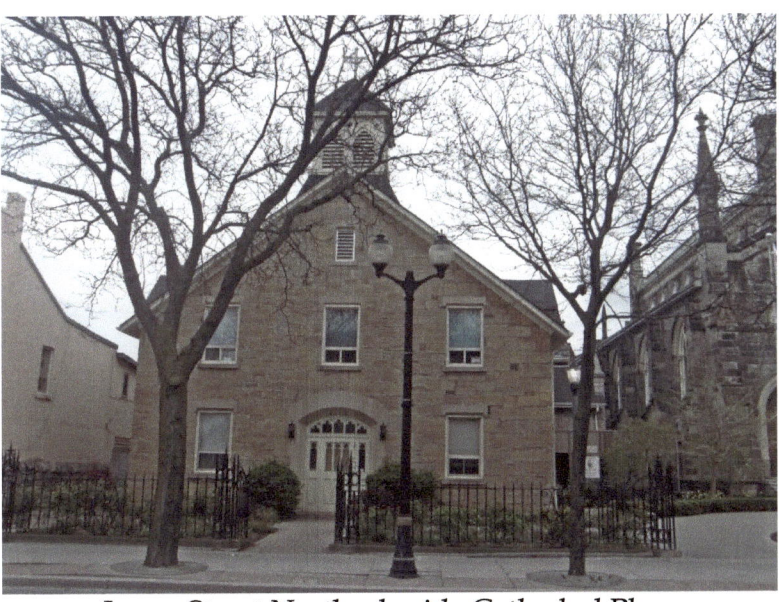

James Street North – beside Cathedral Place
Gothic Revival with cupola

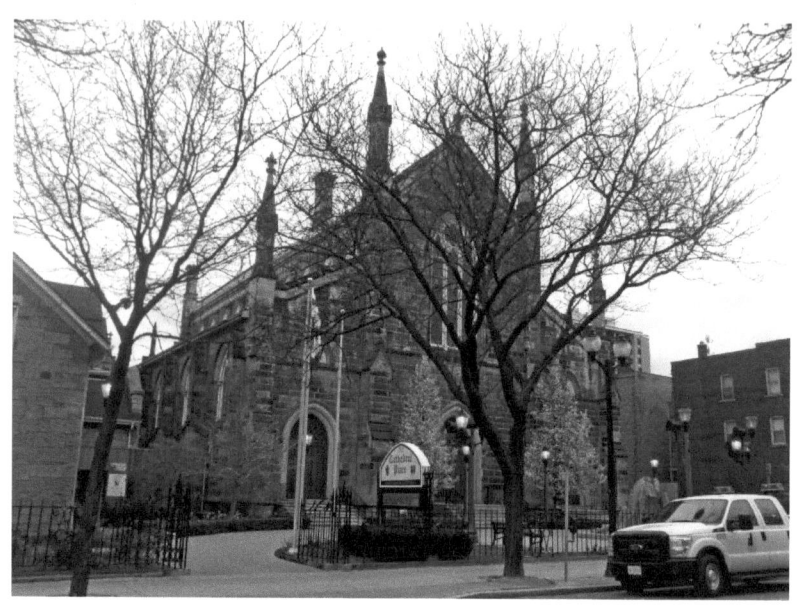

252 James Street North - Cathedral Place – Anglican Church
buttresses

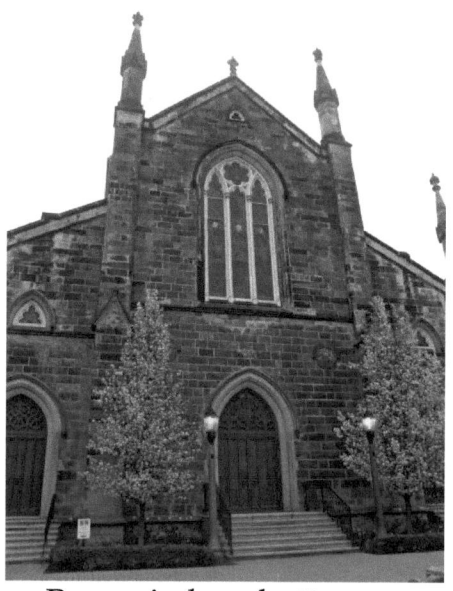

Rose window, buttresses

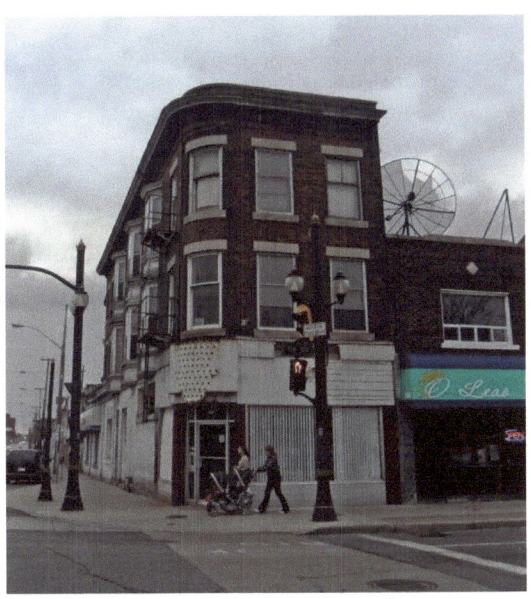

James Street North

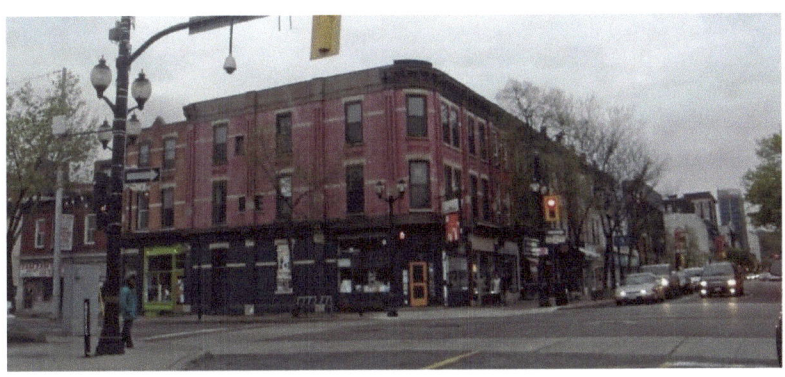

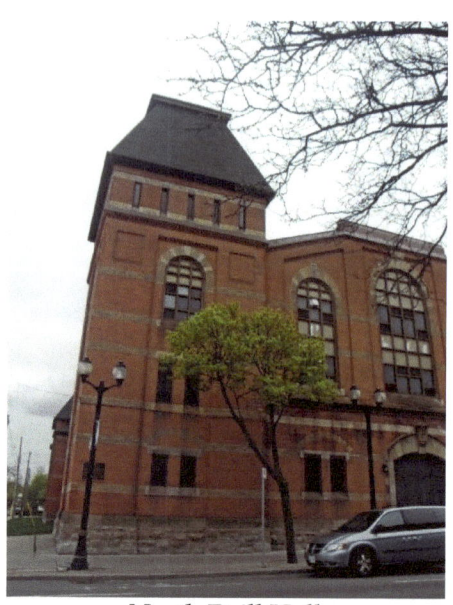

North Drill Hall
Built to house the XIIIth Battalion of Volunteer Militia, it replaced a wooden shed located near this spot which was destroyed in a fire on May 23, 1886. This building was first occupied by the regiment on December 1, 1887. The South Drill Hall was built in 1908. In 1927 the XIIIth became The Royal Hamilton Light Infantry.

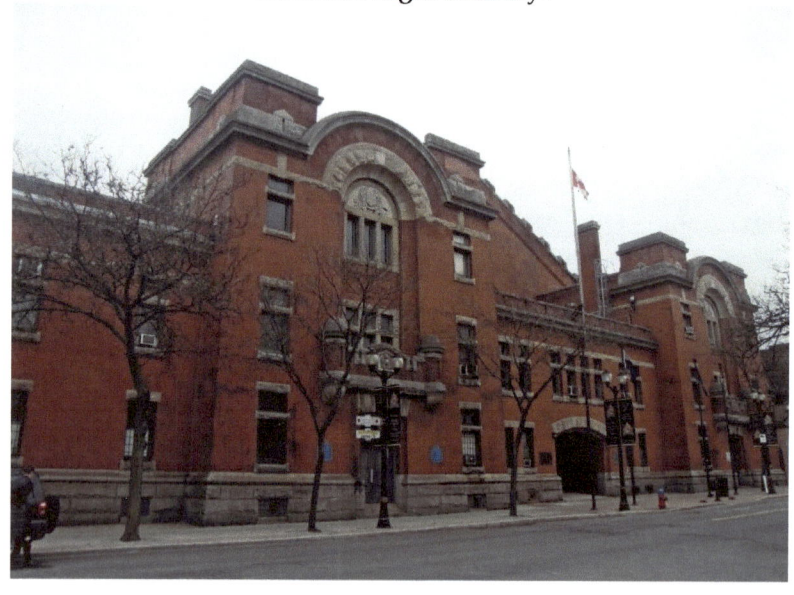

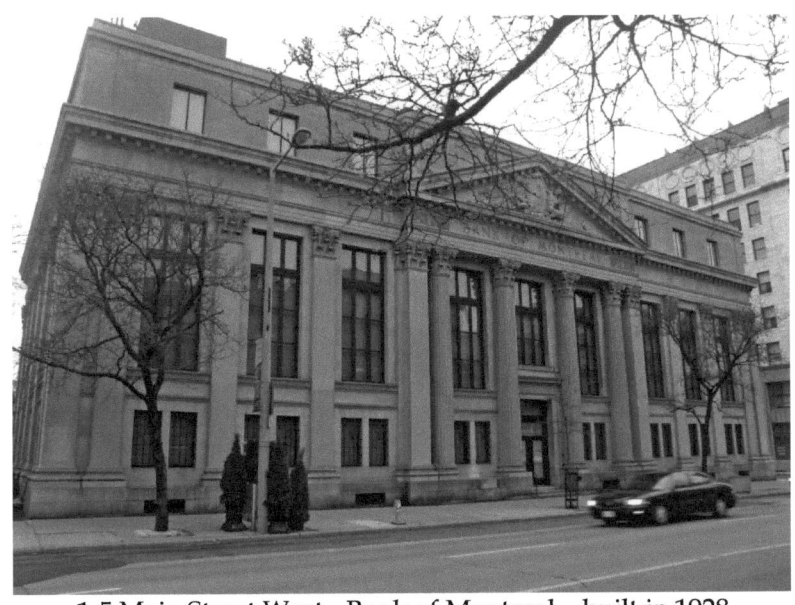

1-5 Main Street West - Bank of Montreal – built in 1928
Two storey building in the Neo-Classical style features four graceful
Corinthian columns and a pediment featuring an intricately carved Bank
of Montreal coat of arms in the tympanum.

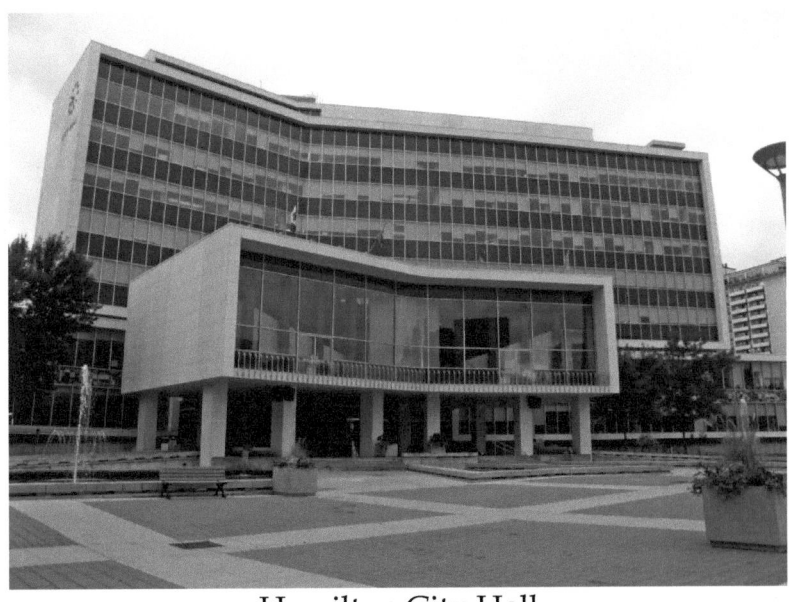

Hamilton City Hall
Main Street West

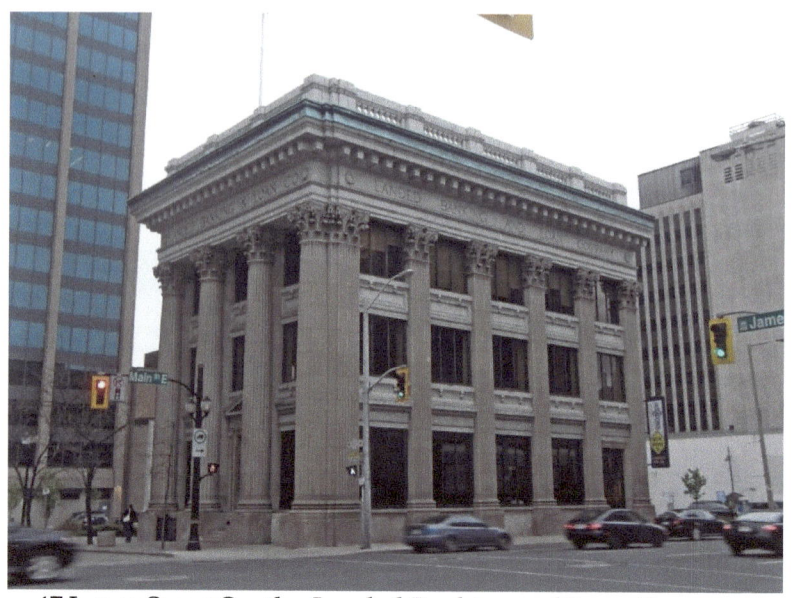

47 James Street South - Landed Banking and Loan Company
Erected in 1908 in the Classical Revival style with its soaring columns
designed to look like an ancient Greek temple – a temple dedicated to
commerce.

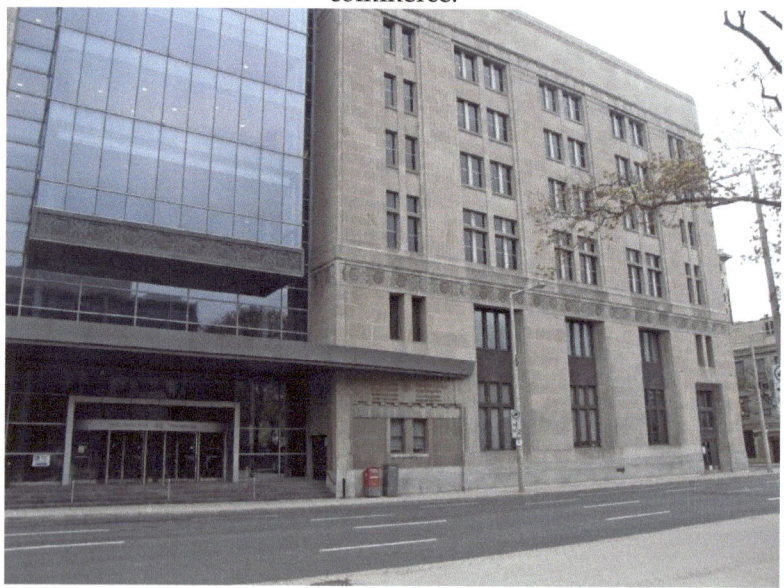

John Sopinka Court House, 45 Main Street East – Provincial Courts
Dominion Public Building erected in 1935-36 housed the Post Office,
customs, and all other government offices until the 1980s.

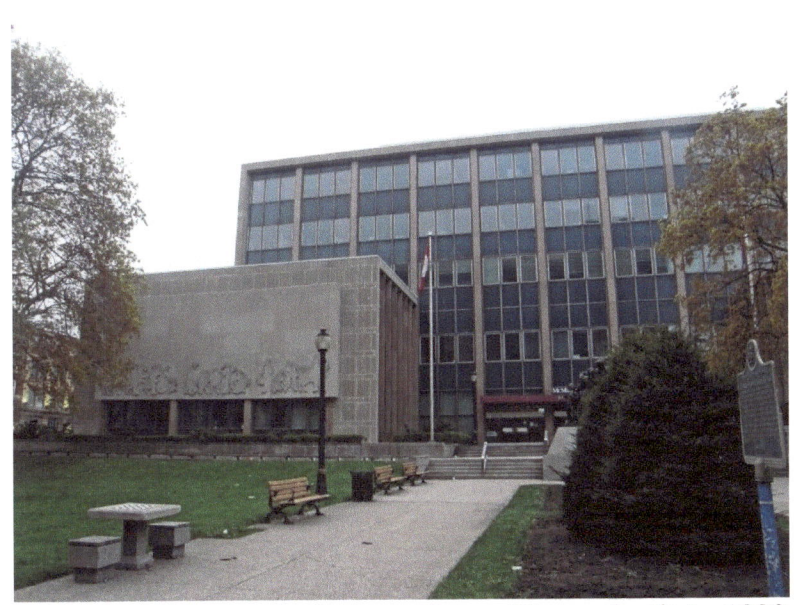

Former Wentworth County Court House built in 1929
Now a McMaster University building
The original courthouse was built in 1878; demolished in 1956.

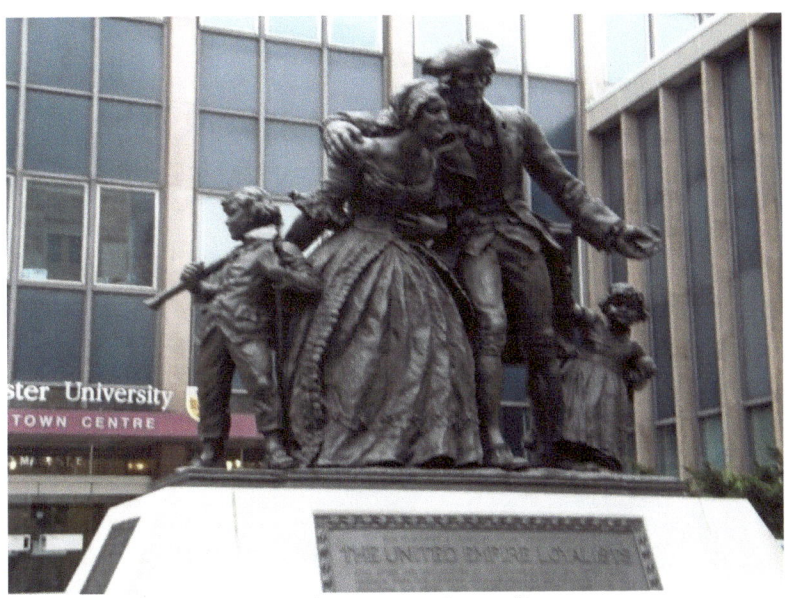

United Empire Loyalists

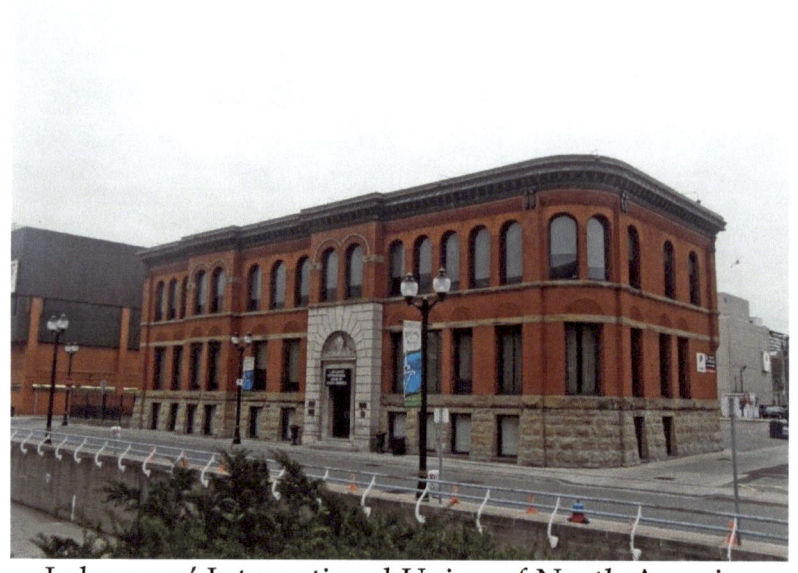

Labourers' International Union of North America
44 Hughson Street South

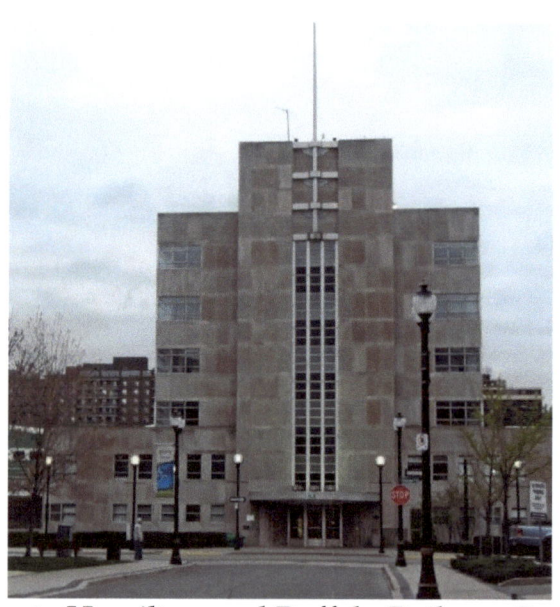

Toronto Hamilton and Buffalo Railway Station
Built in 1933 in the Art Deco style – currently GO Station

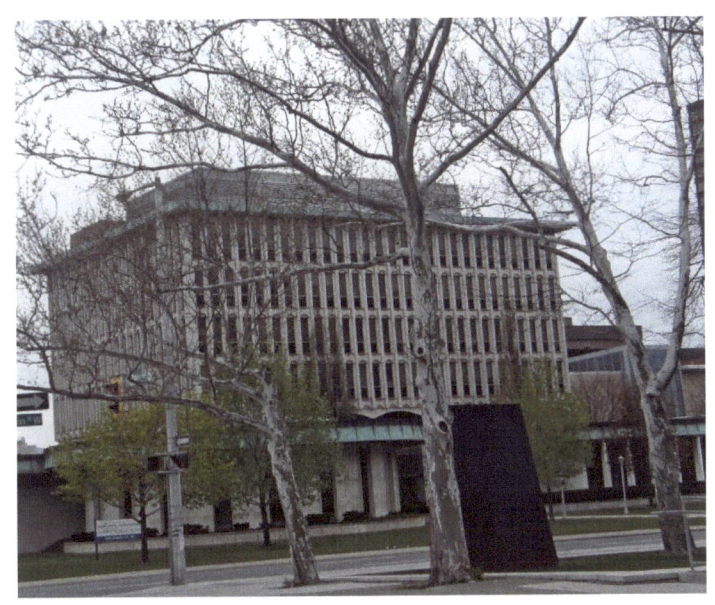

Hamilton Wentworth District School Board
100 Main Street West

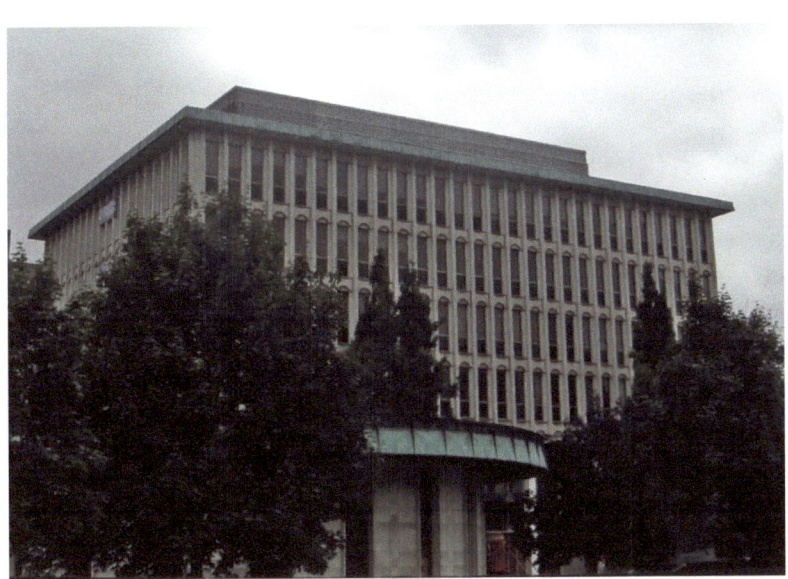

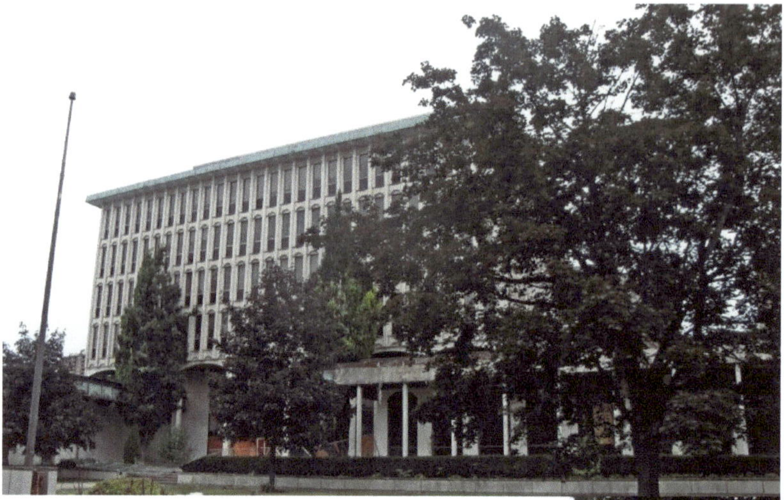

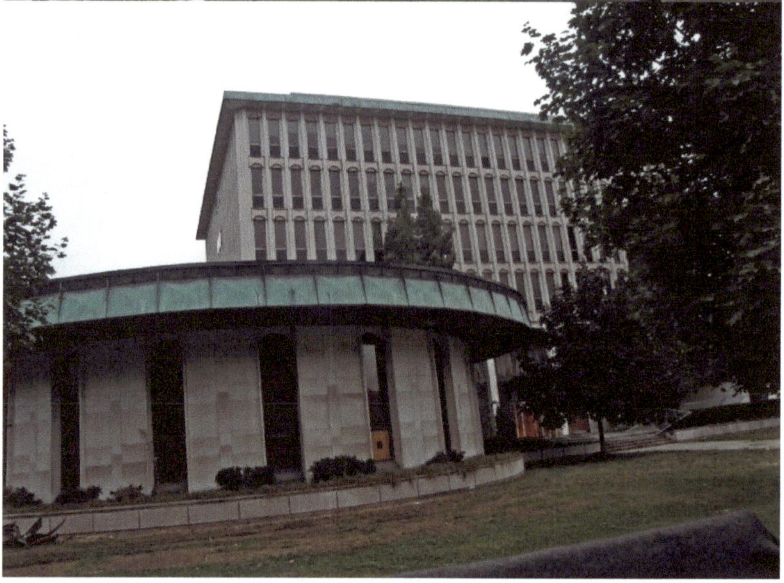

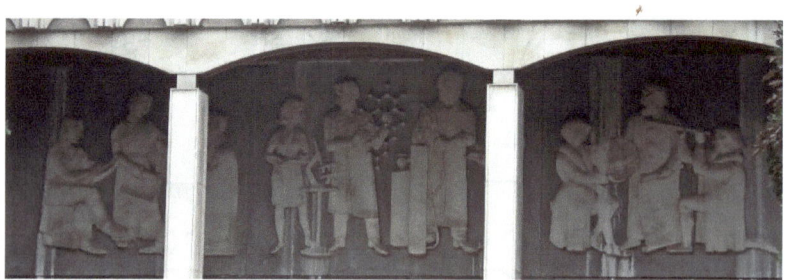

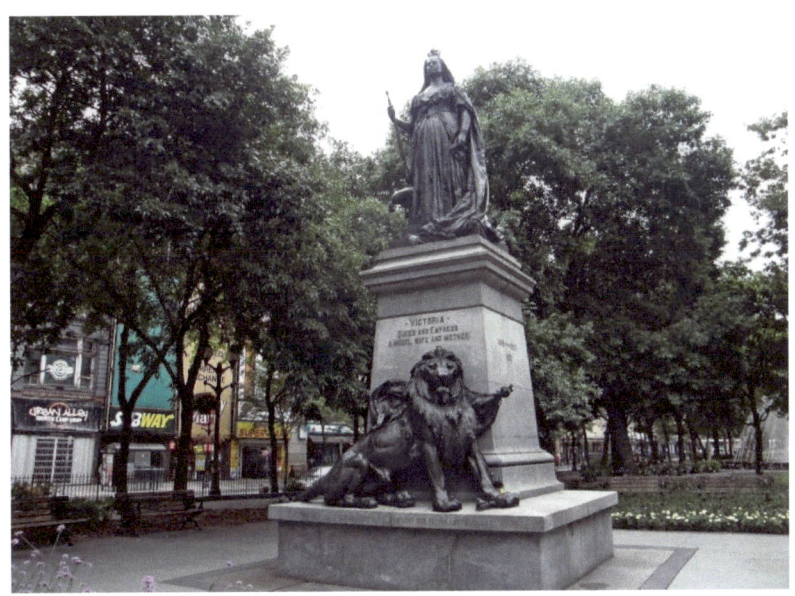

Statute of Queen Victoria in Gore Park

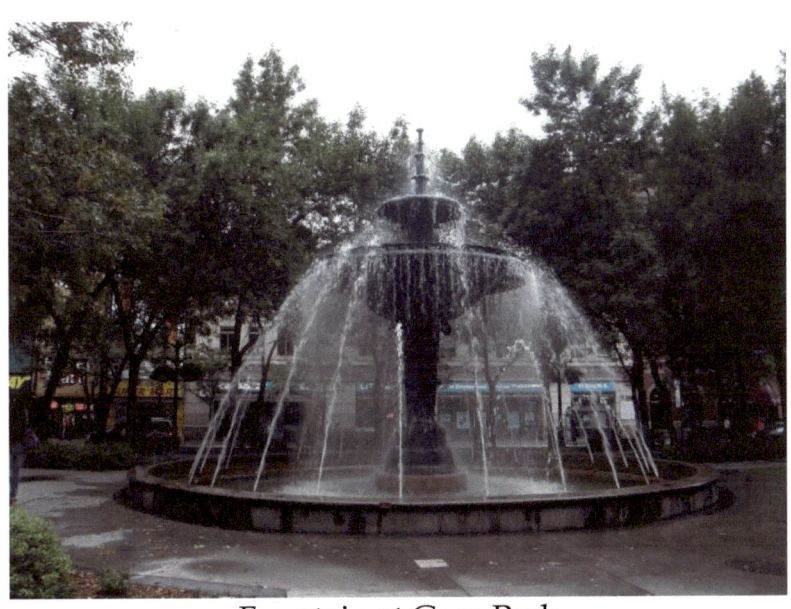

Fountain at Gore Park

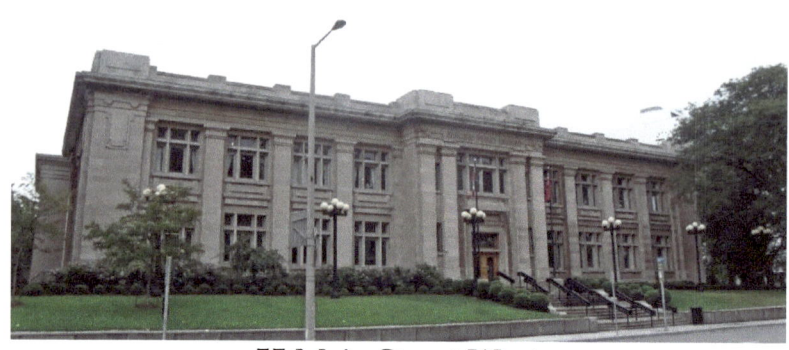

55 Main Street West
Hamilton Public Library was constructed in 1913 in the Beaux
Arts style with pillars, dentil moulding under cornice. It
served as the main library for 67 years. Refurbished in 1989 to
house the Unified Family Court

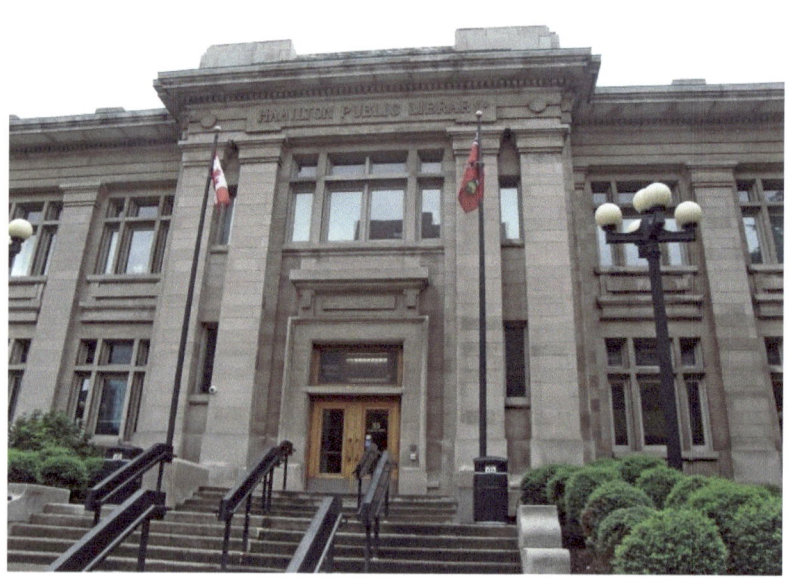

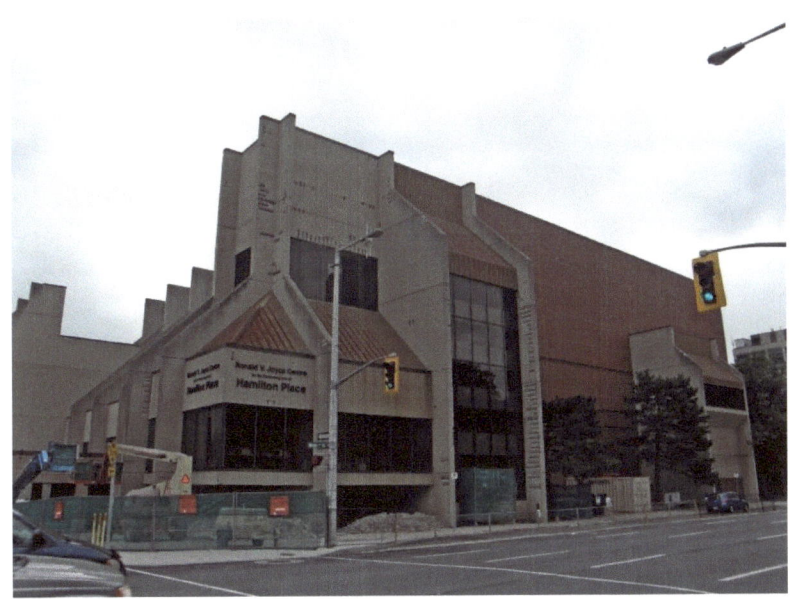

Hamilton Place

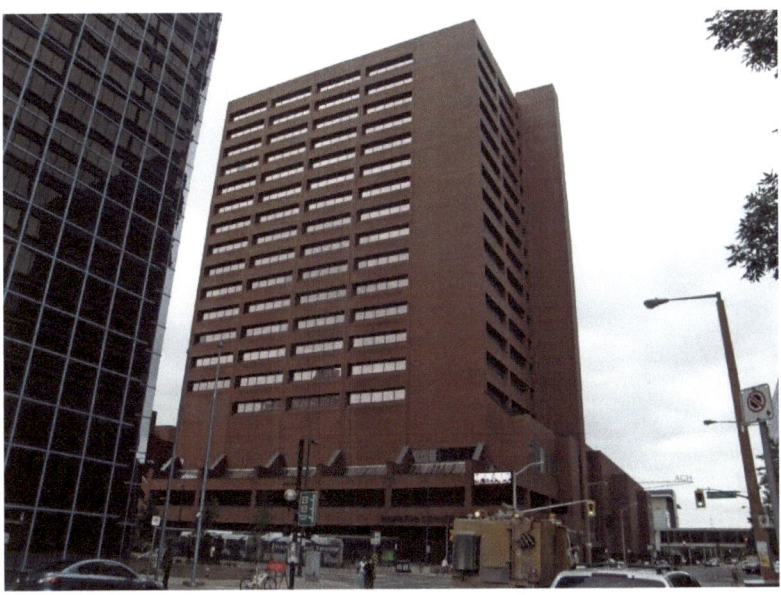

Hamilton Convention Centre

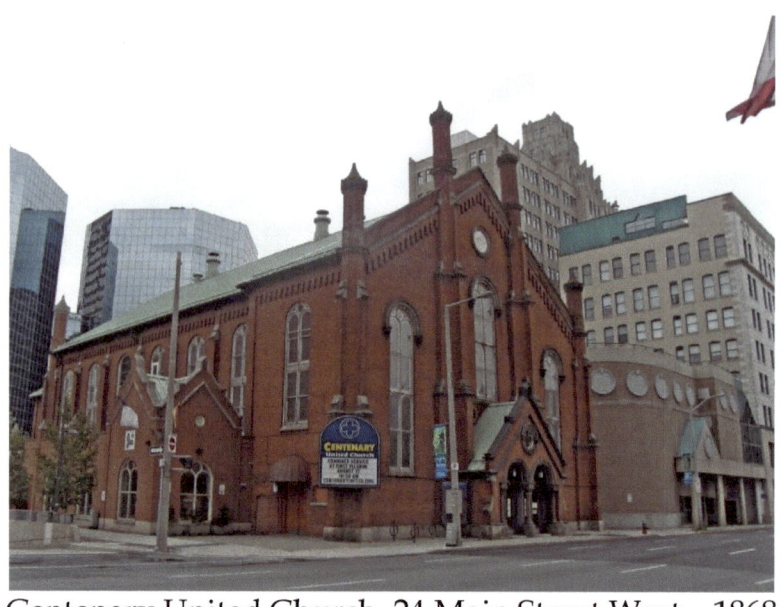

Centenary United Church, 24 Main Street West – 1868
In the Victorian Romanesque style; buttresses,
corbelled dentils

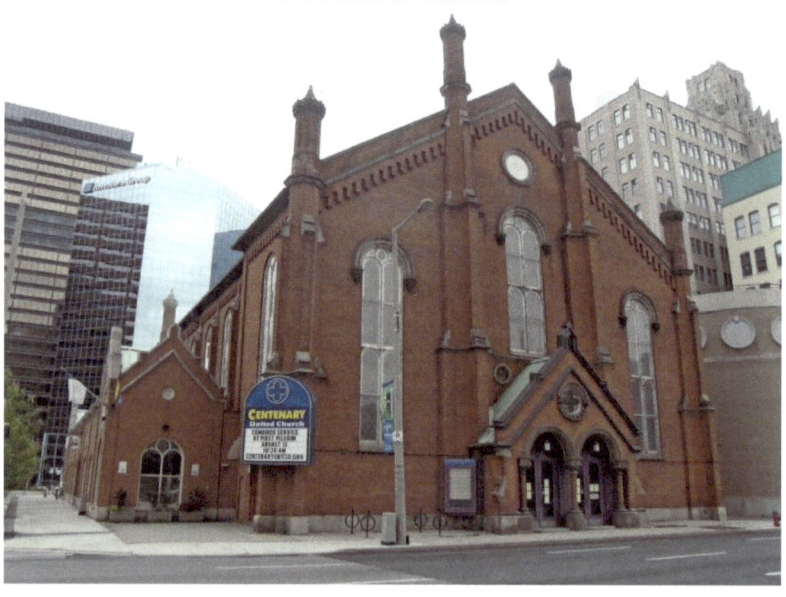

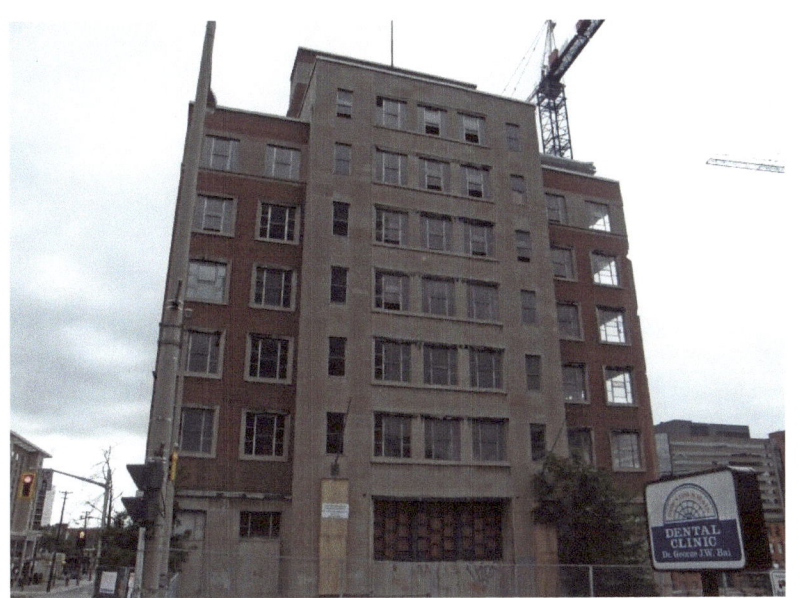

Remains of the Federal Building
Corner of Caroline and Main Streets

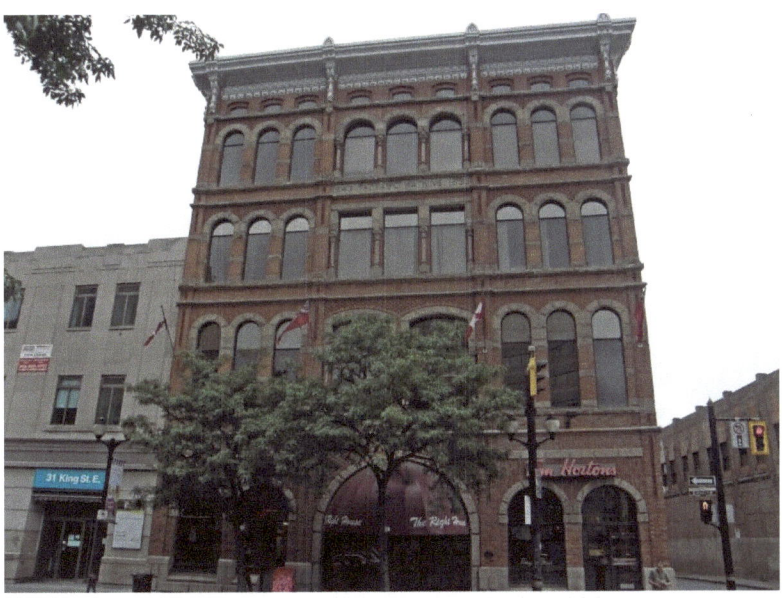

Thomas C. Watkins 1843-1893
The Right House – corner of King and Hughson Streets

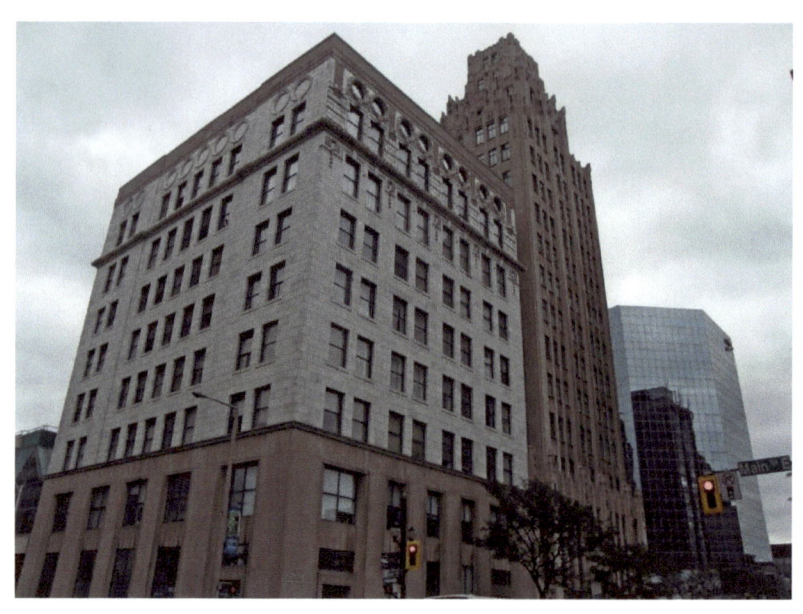

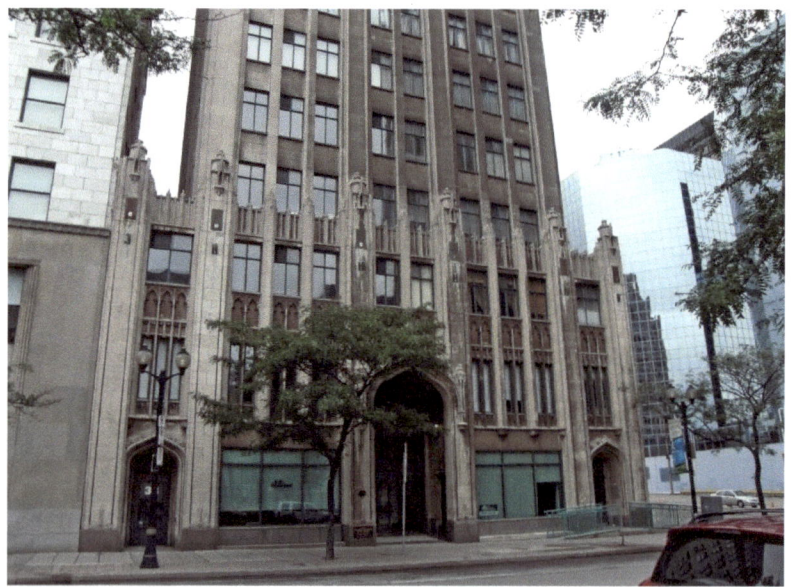

Art Deco style

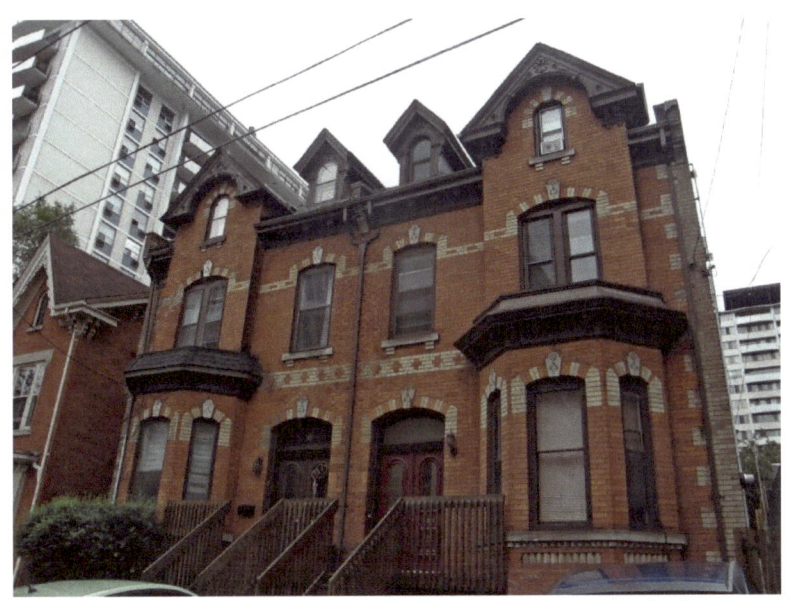

119-121 Jackson Street West – Gothic Revival, dichromatic brickwork, dormers in attic, bay windows

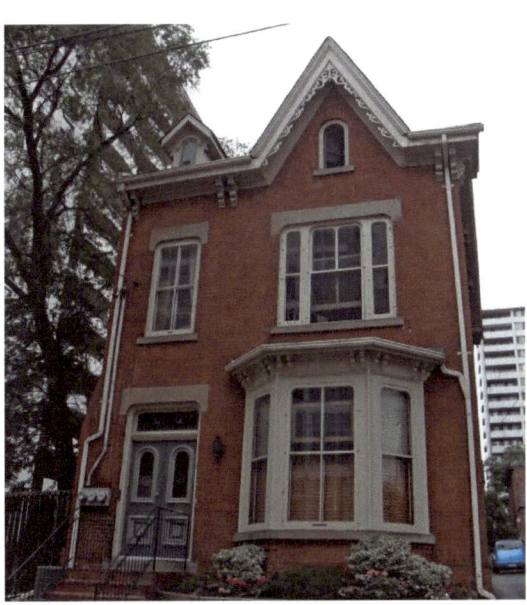

123 Jackson Street West – Gothic Revival, dormer in attic, bay window

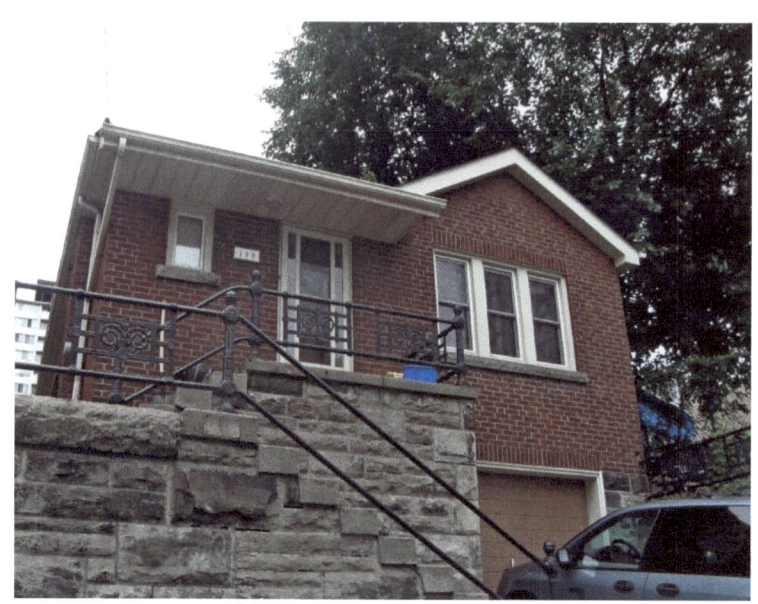

129 Jackson Street West

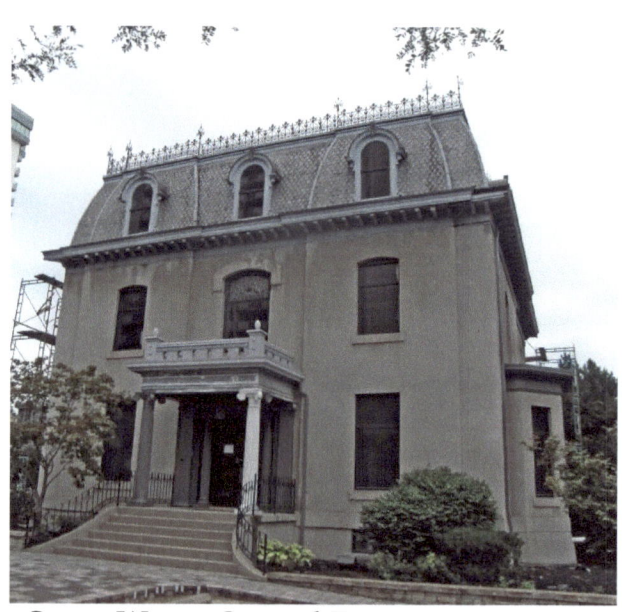

Jackson Street West – Second Empire, mansard roof, iron cresting, fish scale tiles, ionic capitals on pillars

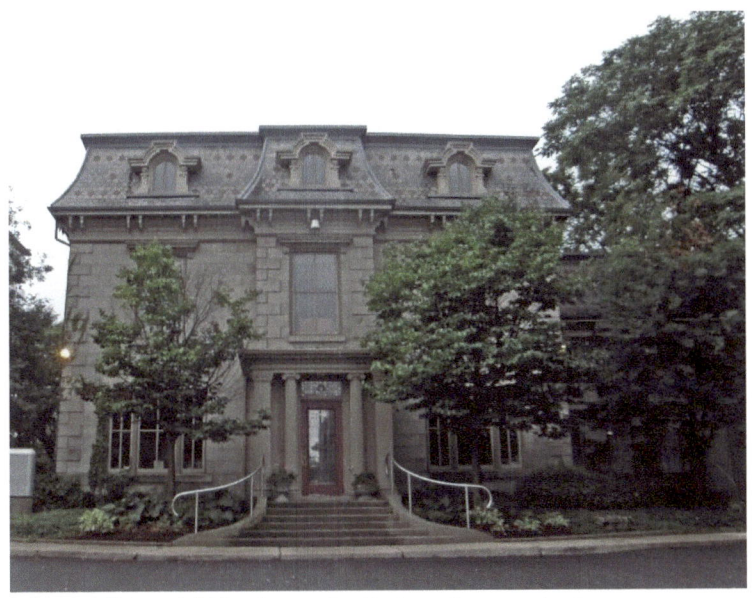

163 Jackson Street West was built for pharmacist/entrepreneur
Tristram Bickle c. 1850 – Second Empire style, mansard roof, dichromatic
tile work; ionic capitals on pillars, cornice brackets, corner quoins. Bishop
T.B. Fuller moved here in 1884. From 1892 to 1932, Southam newspapers
owner William Southam lived here. In 1954, Ken Soble launched CHCH
TV here.

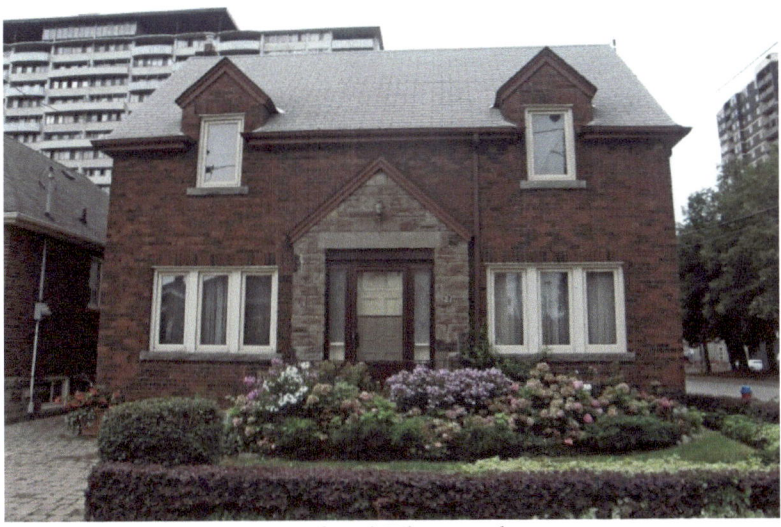

21 Wesanford Place - dormers

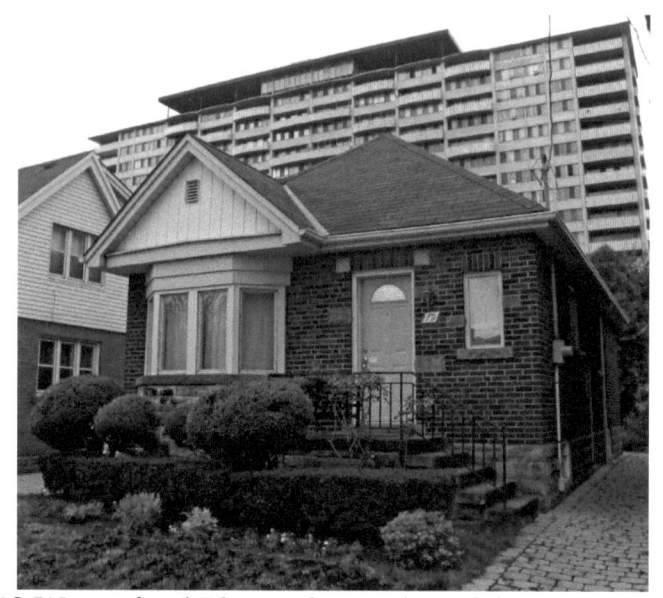

19 Wesanford Place – hipped roof, bay window

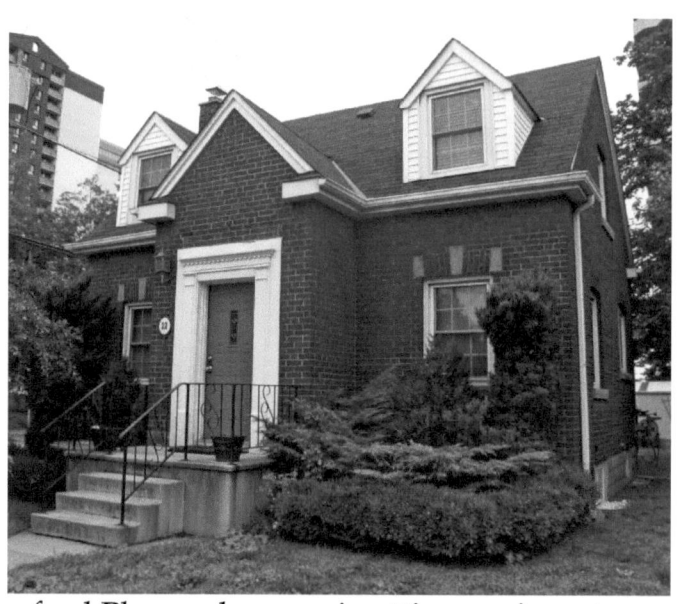

22 Wesanford Place – dormers in attic, cornice return on gable

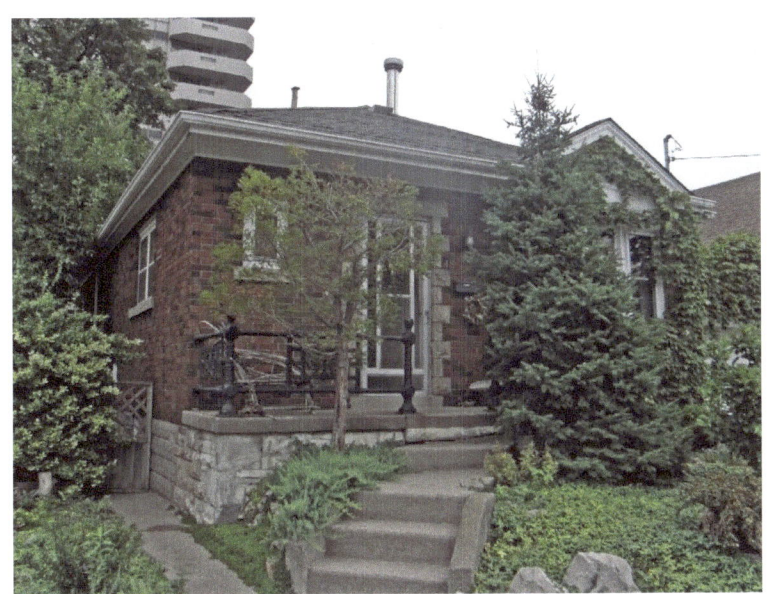

18 Wesanford Place

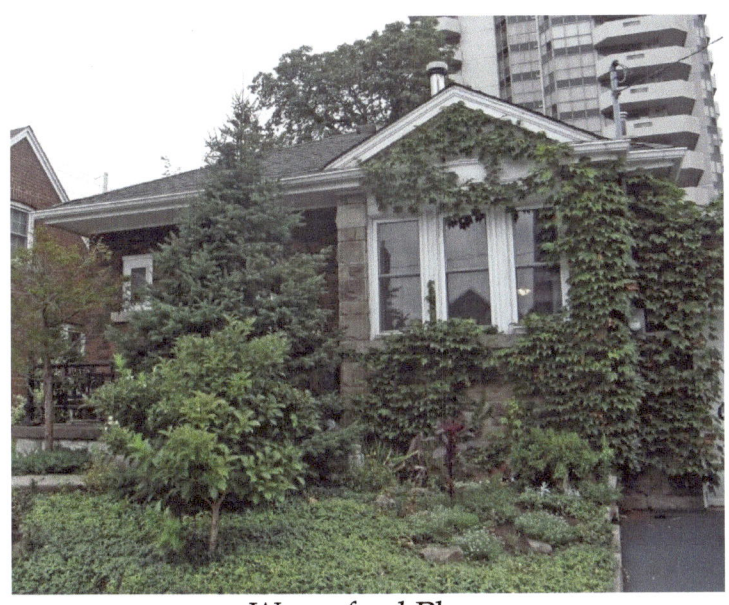

Wesanford Place

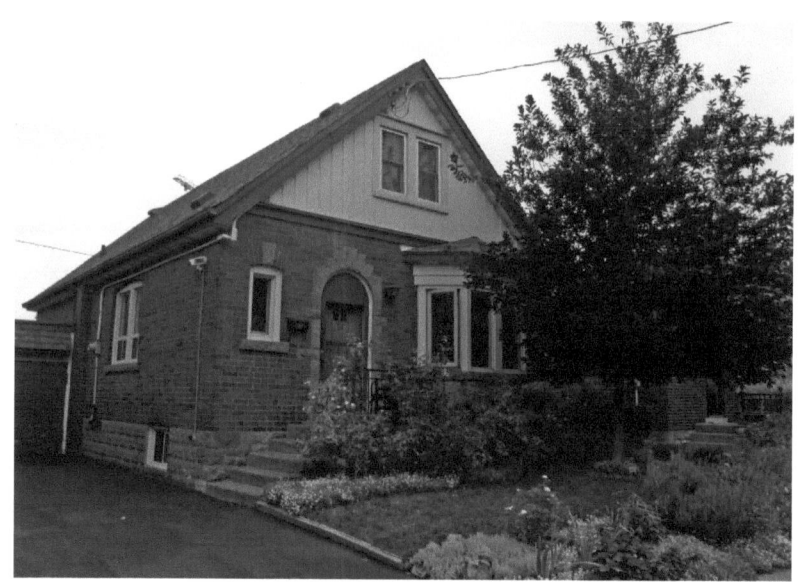

14 Wesanford Place – Gothic Revival, bay window

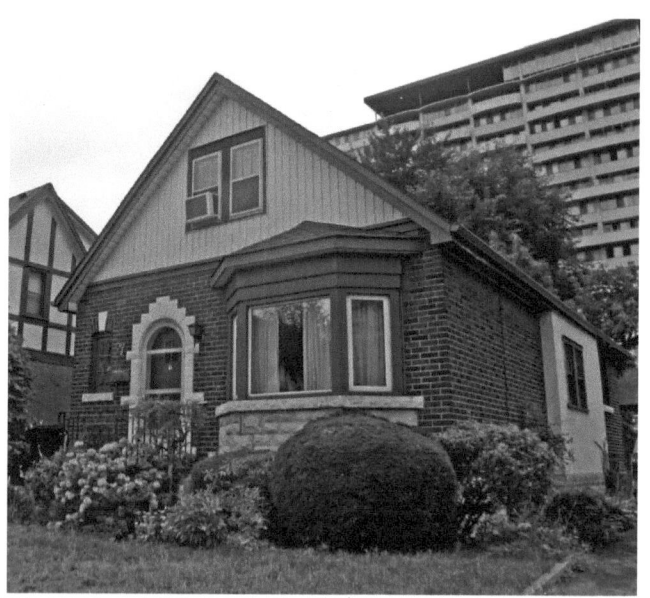

7 Wesanford Place – Gothic Revival, bay window

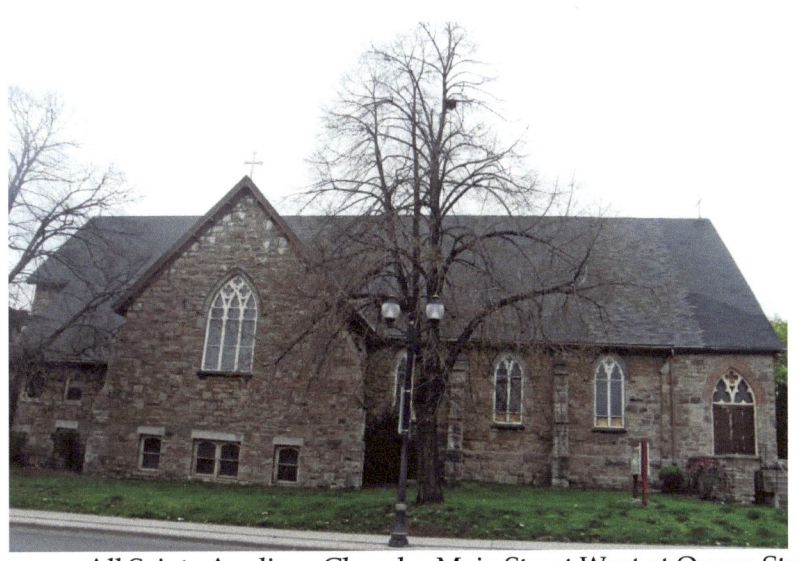

All Saints Anglican Church - Main Street West at Queen Street
Building began in 1872 and had a large tower
The support stones for the tower were damaged by a 5.4 earthquake on
September 24, 1998 and the spire was removed.
In the fall of 2009, the church was declared unsafe with pieces of the roof
falling into the nave.

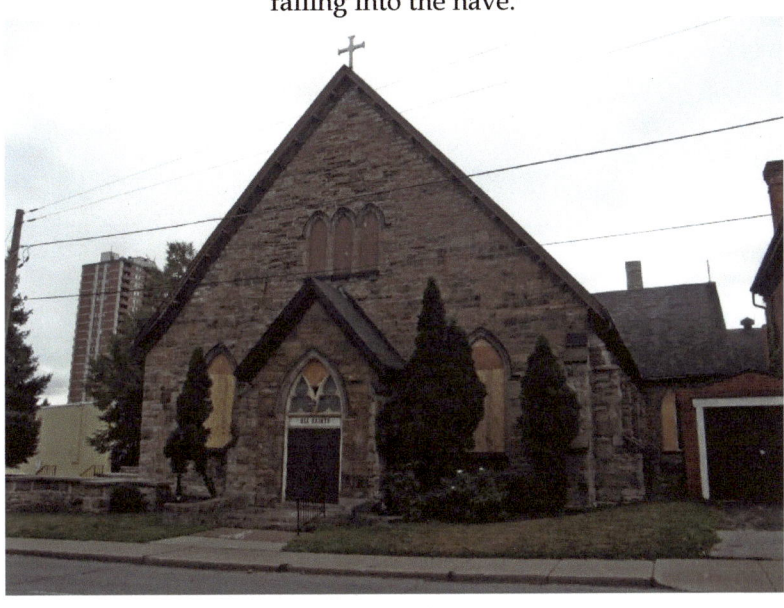

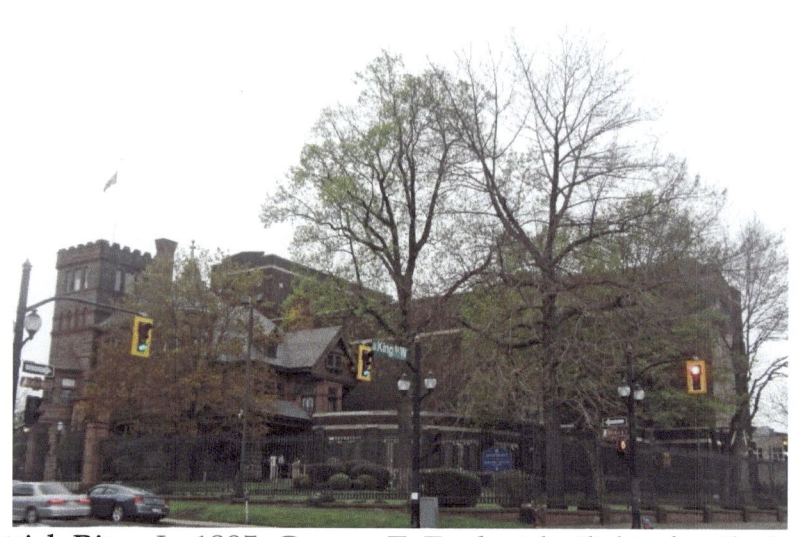

Scottish Rite - In 1895, George T. Tuckett built his family home known as "The Towers," which now forms the Club portion of The Scottish Rite building. The property was used as a military headquarters and hospital during World War One, and was then acquired by The Scottish Rite Masons in 1920. The Cathedral portion of the building was built over the winter of 1922 to 1923.

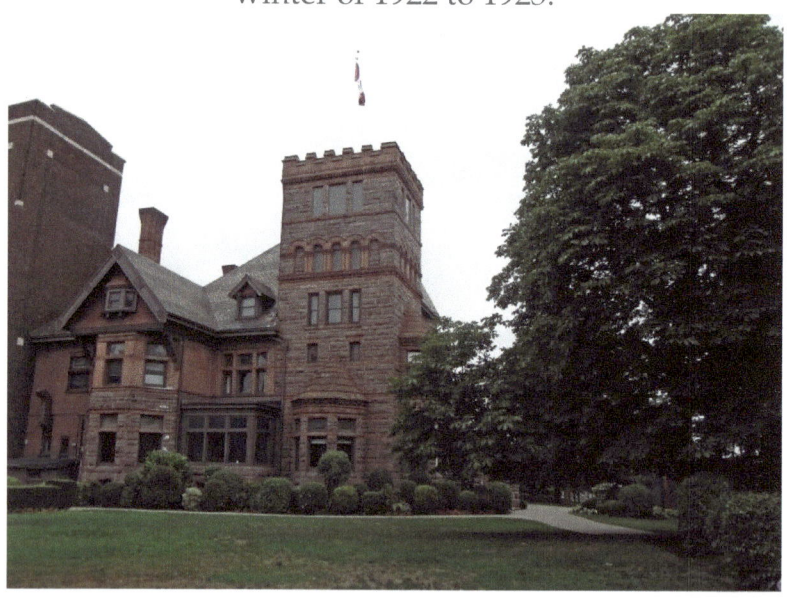

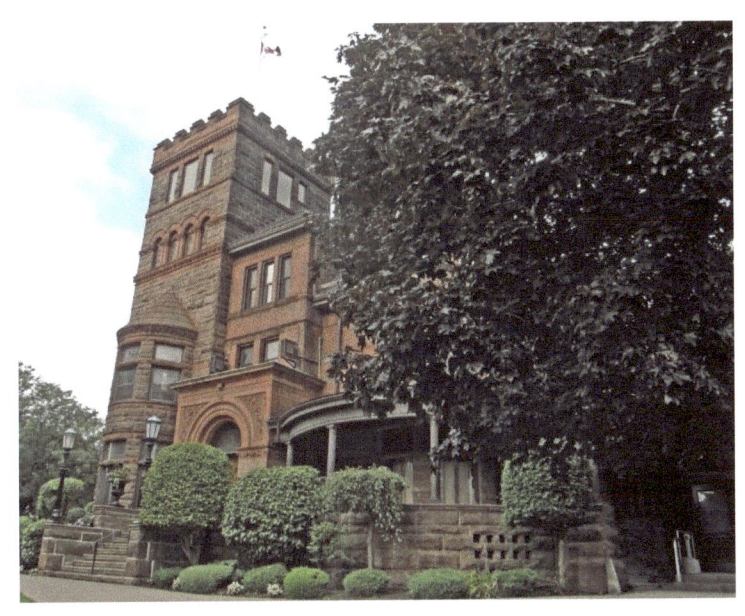

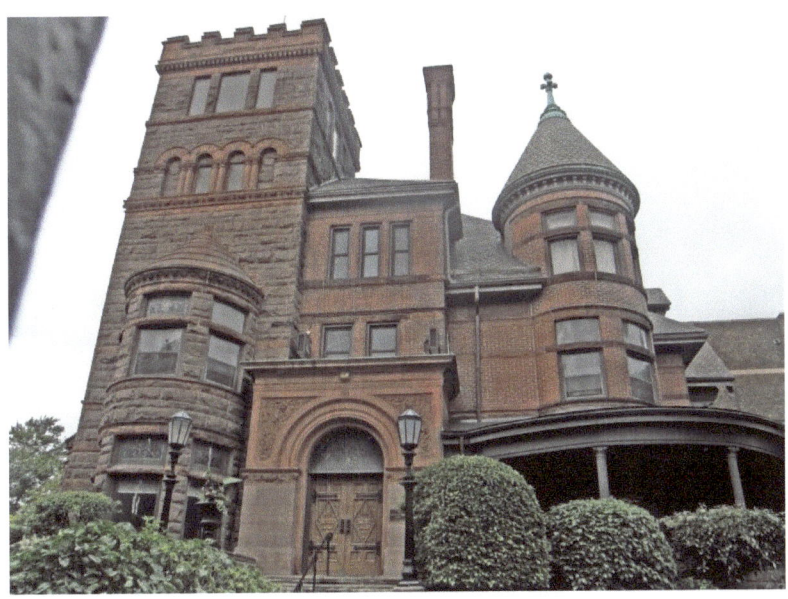

turret

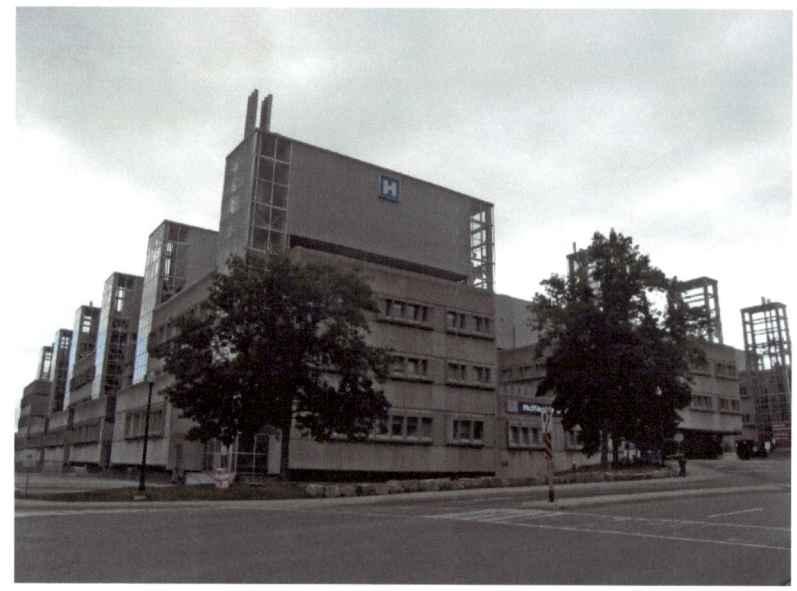

McMaster Children's Hospital

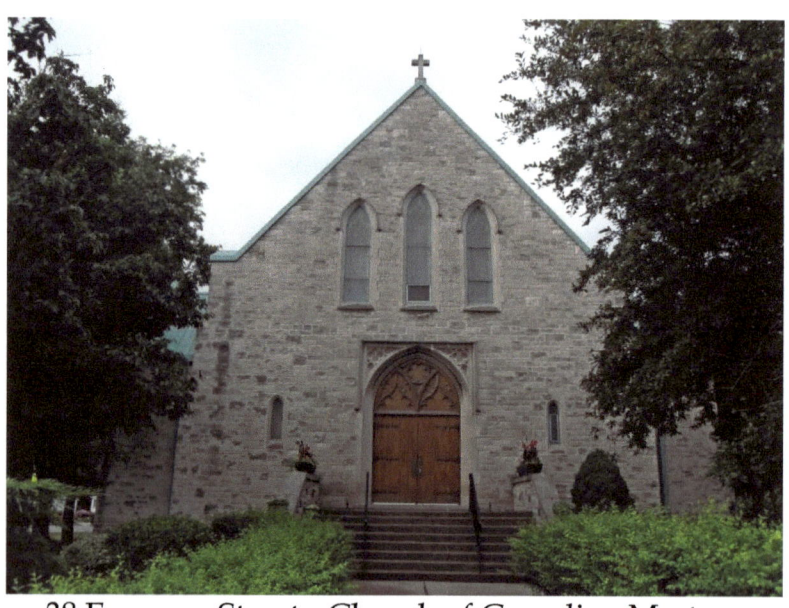

38 Emerson Street - Church of Canadian Martyrs

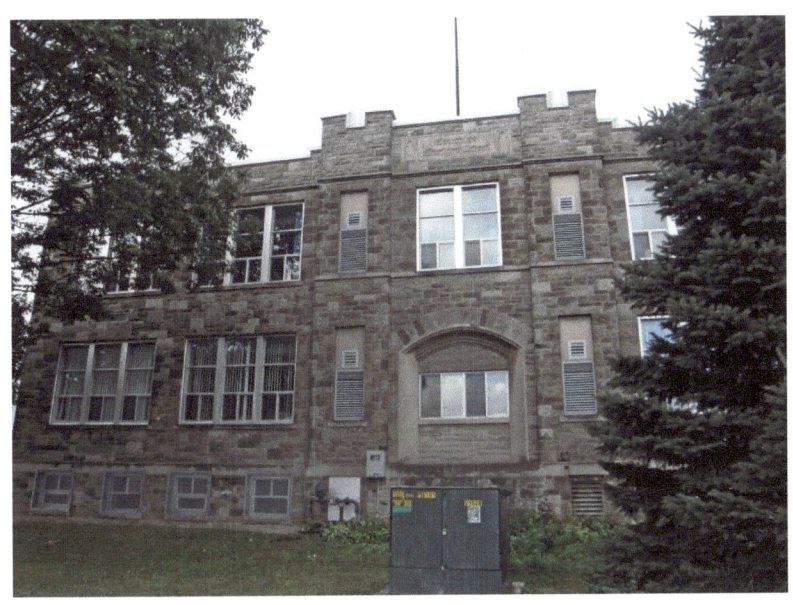

1355 Main Street West
Canadian Martyrs Catholic Elementary School

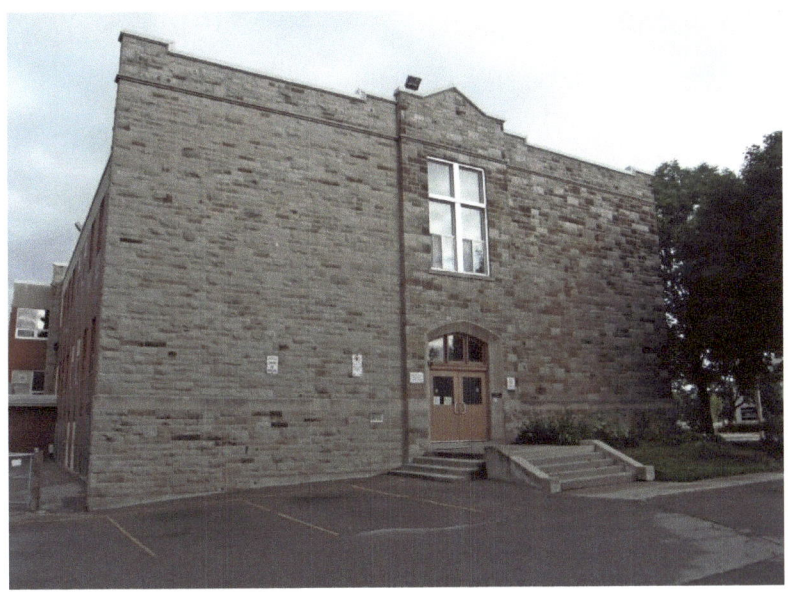

limestone

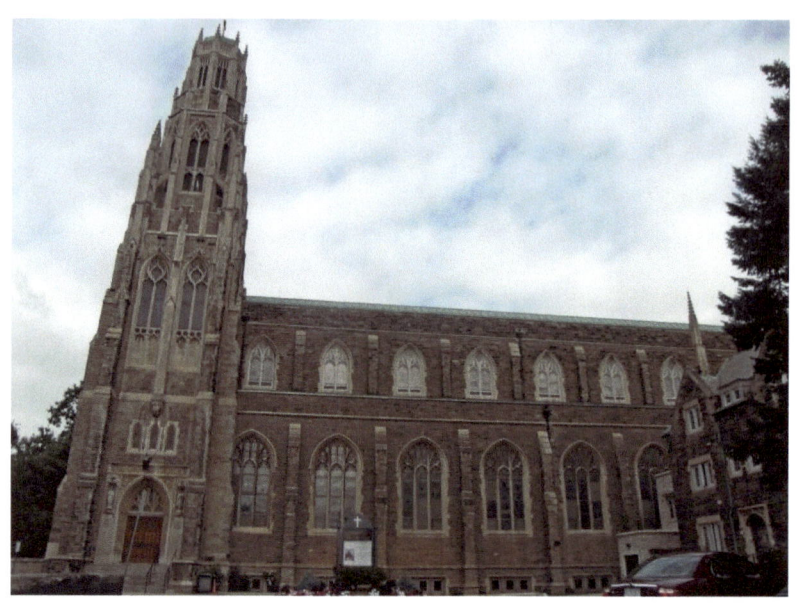

Basilica of Christ the King, Gothic style
Built 1931-33

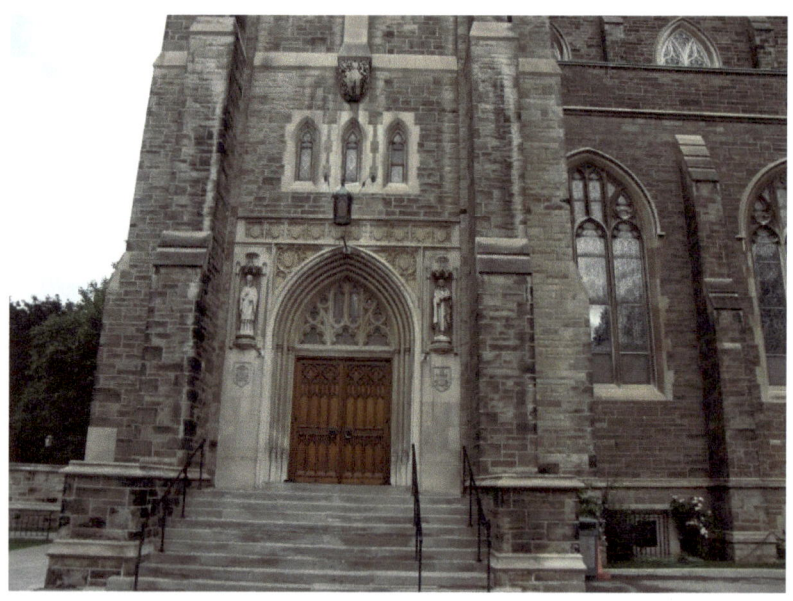

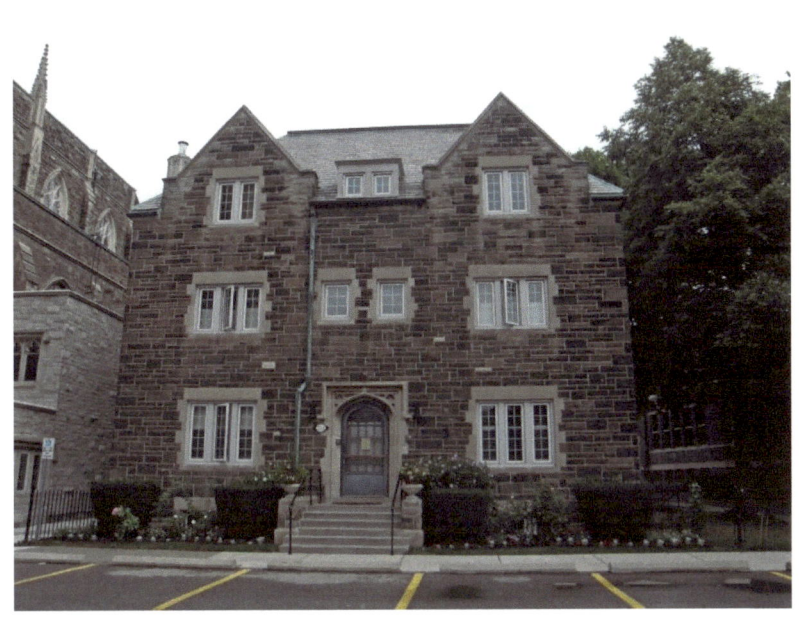

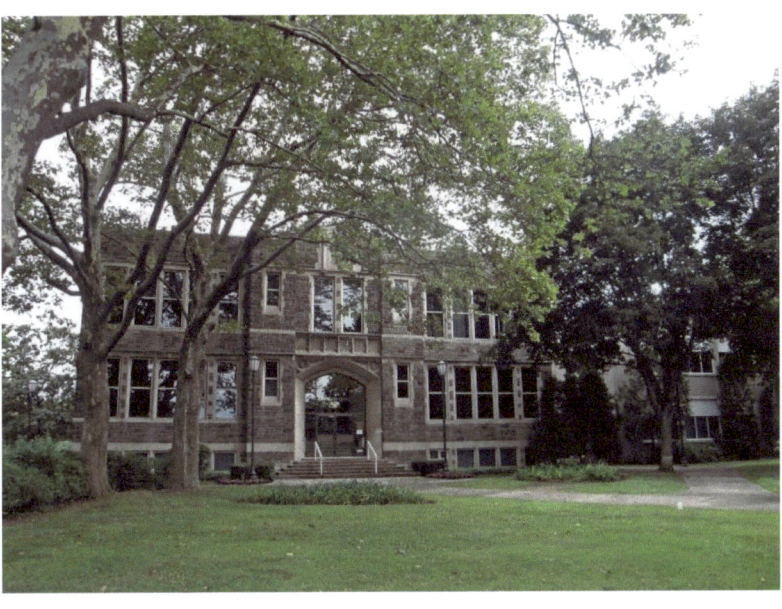

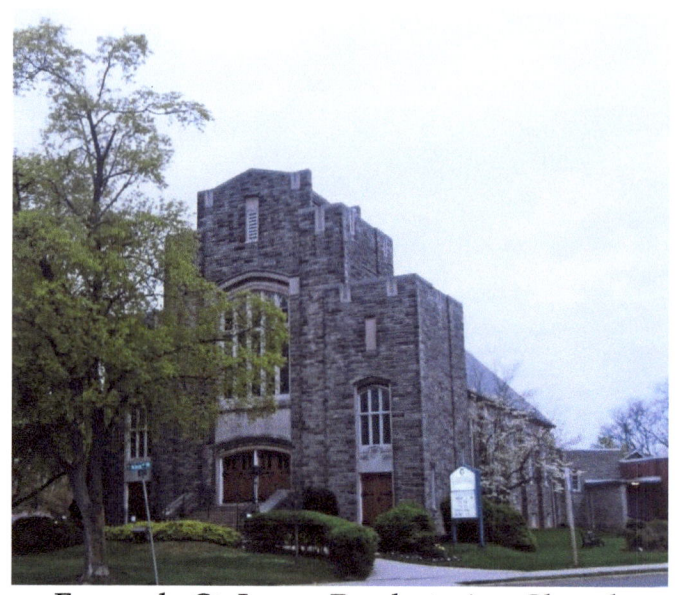

Formerly St. James Presbyterian Church
Now MacNeil Baptist Church 1145 King Street West

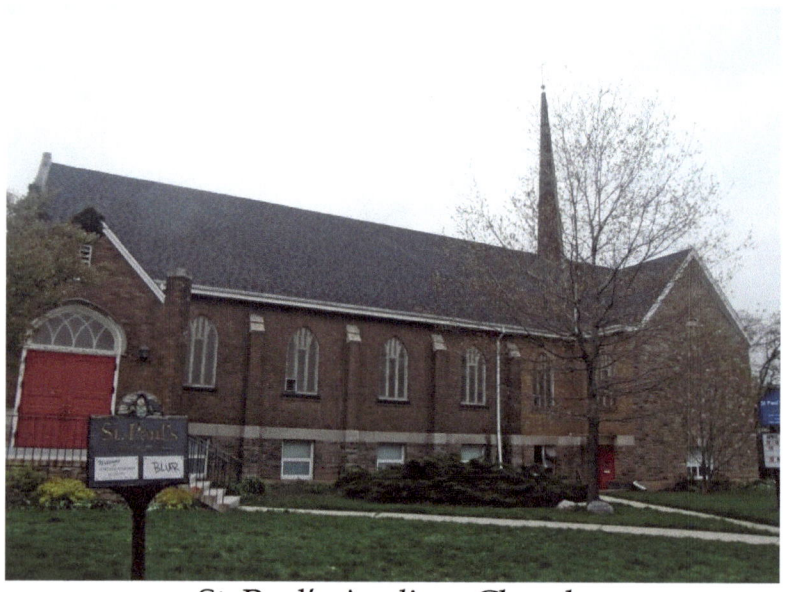

St. Paul's Anglican Church
1140 King Street West

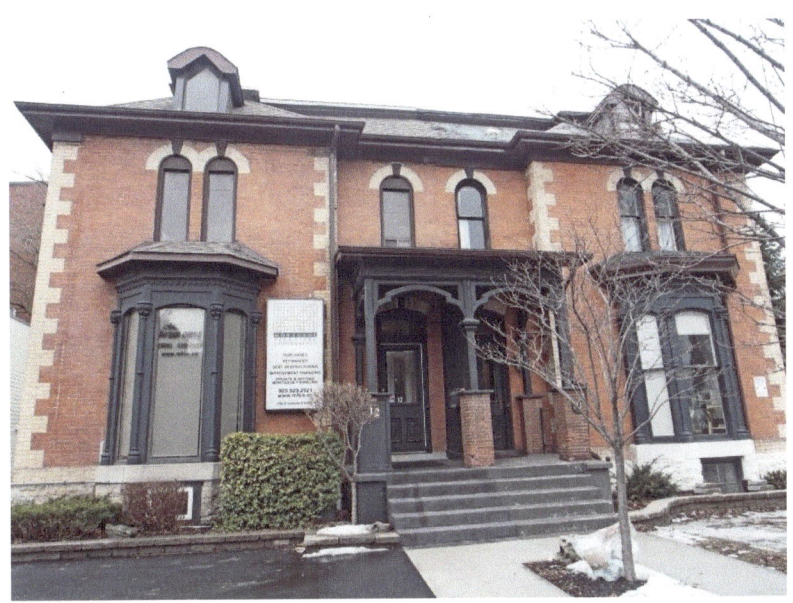

10-12 Ray Street – Italianate, dormers, corner quoins, keystones and voussoirs, bay windows

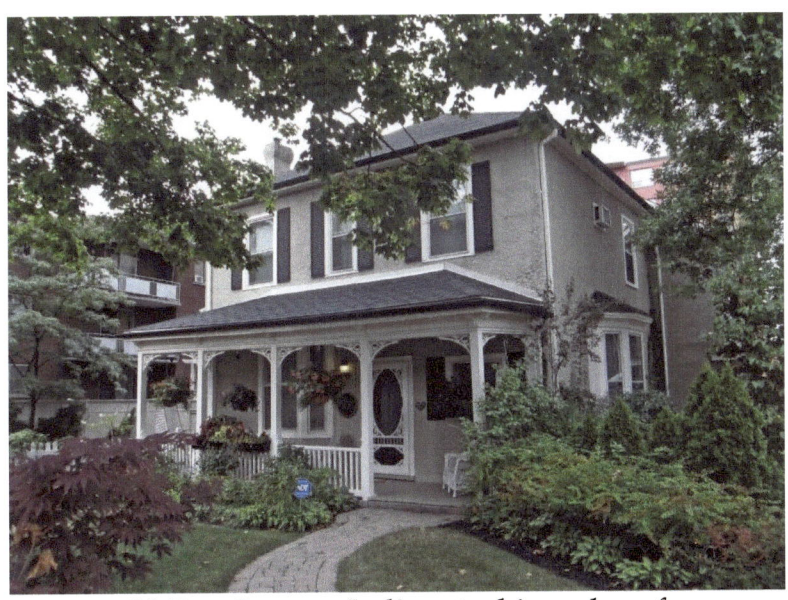

28 Ray Street – Italianate, hipped roof

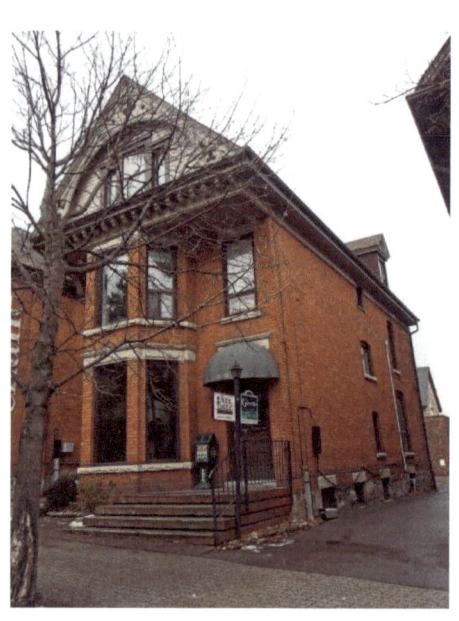

108 George Street – Edwardian, Palladian window,
two-storey bay window

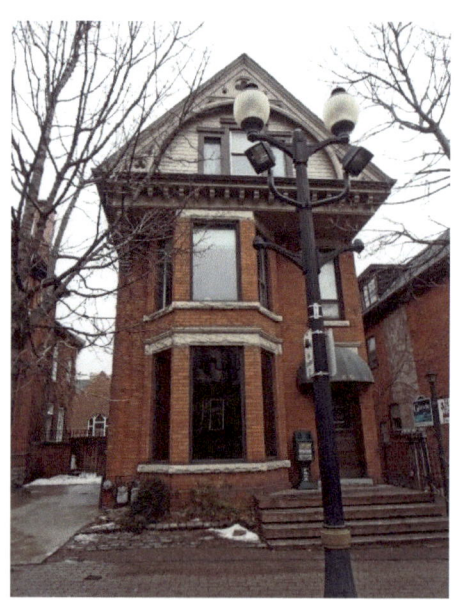

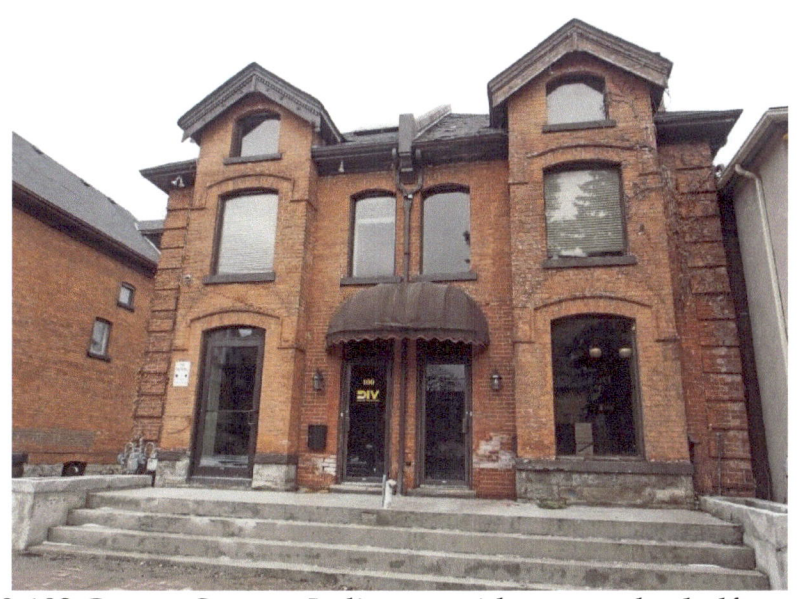

100-102 George Street – Italianate with two-and-a-half storey tower-like bays

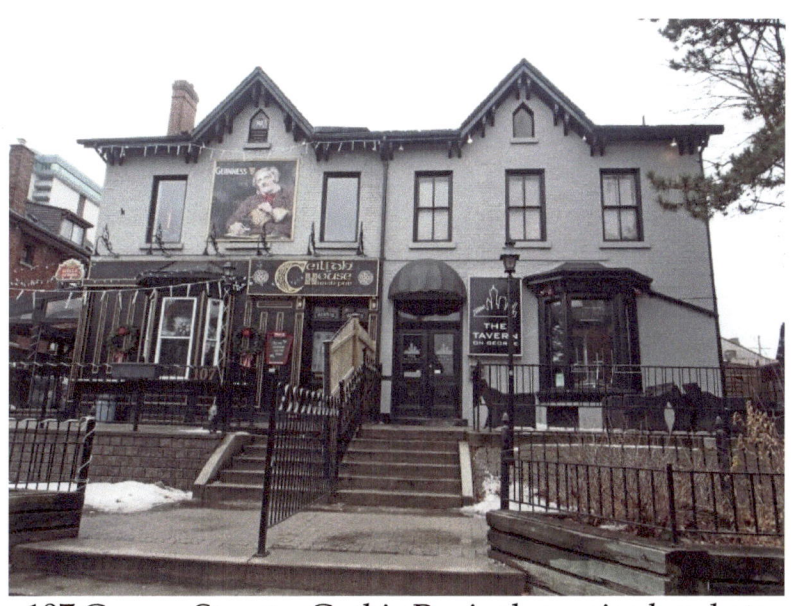

107 George Street – Gothic Revival, cornice brackets

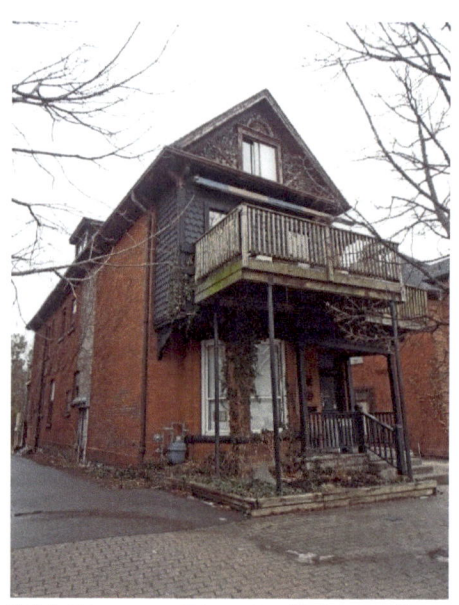

104 George Street - Edwardian

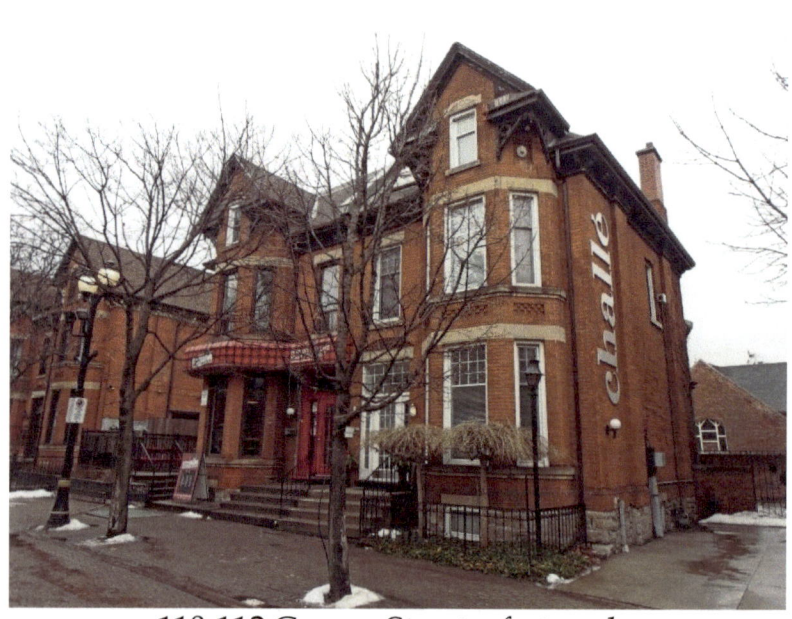

110-112 George Street – fretwork,
two-and-a-half storey tower-like bays

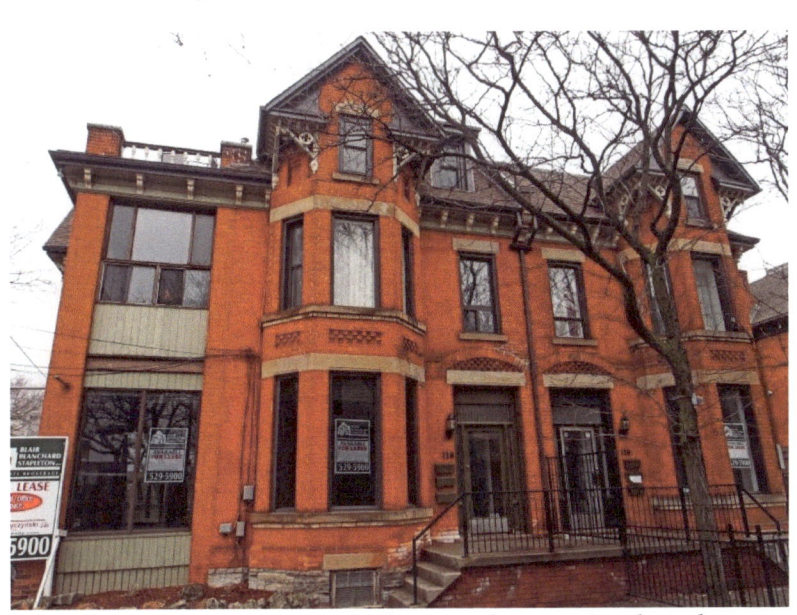

116-118 George Street – fretwork, cornice brackets, two-and-a-half storey tower-like bays

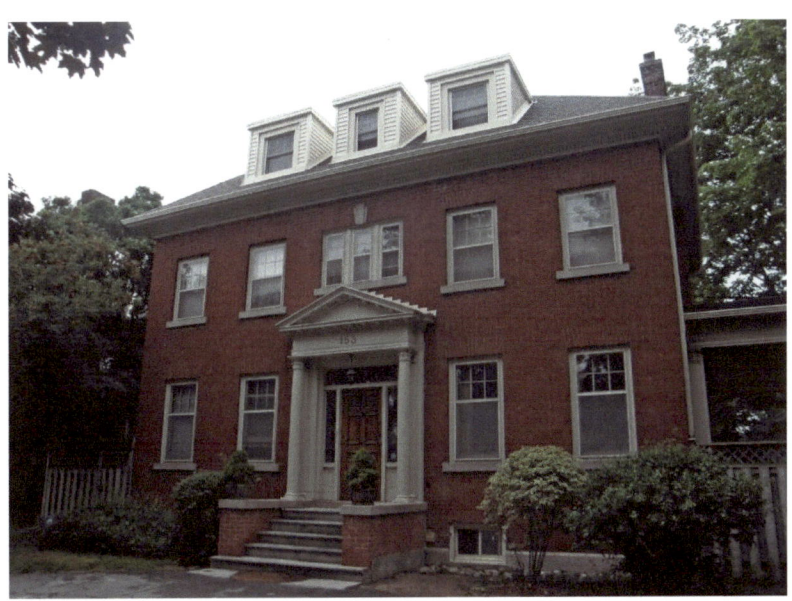

153 George Street – Georgian, dormers in attic, pediment above entrance

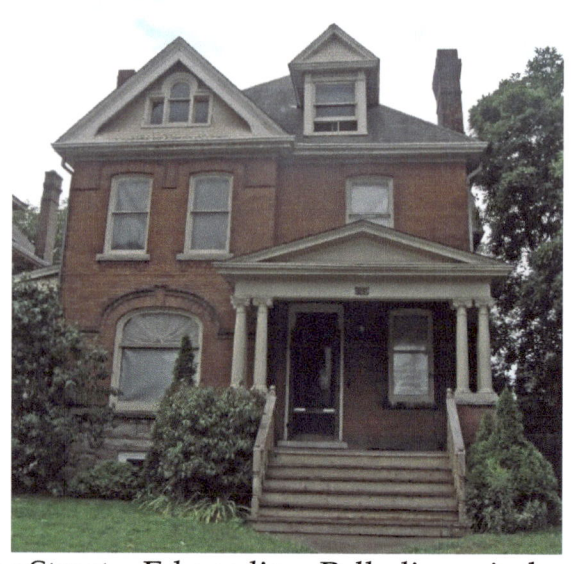

149 George Street – Edwardian, Palladian window, dormer, pediment above porch, Romanesque style window hoods, dentil moulding, ionic capitals on pillars

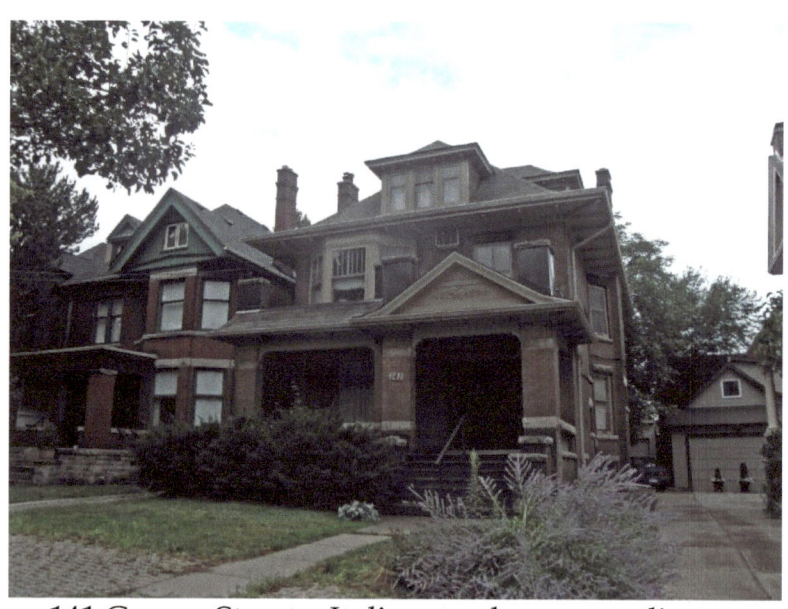

141 George Street – Italianate, dormer, pediment

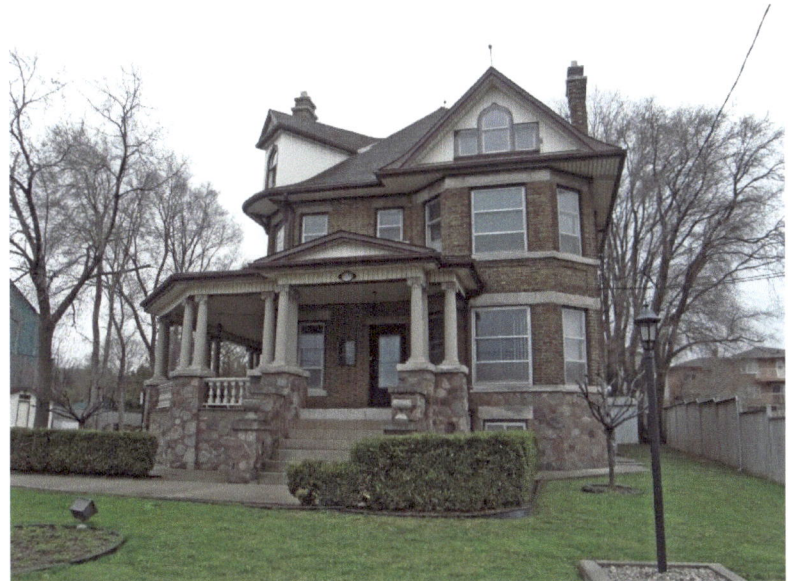

2826 King Street East by former Nash Farm Market –
Edwardian, Palladian window, dormer, wraparound
verandah, pediment, two-storey bay window

Hamilton Mountain

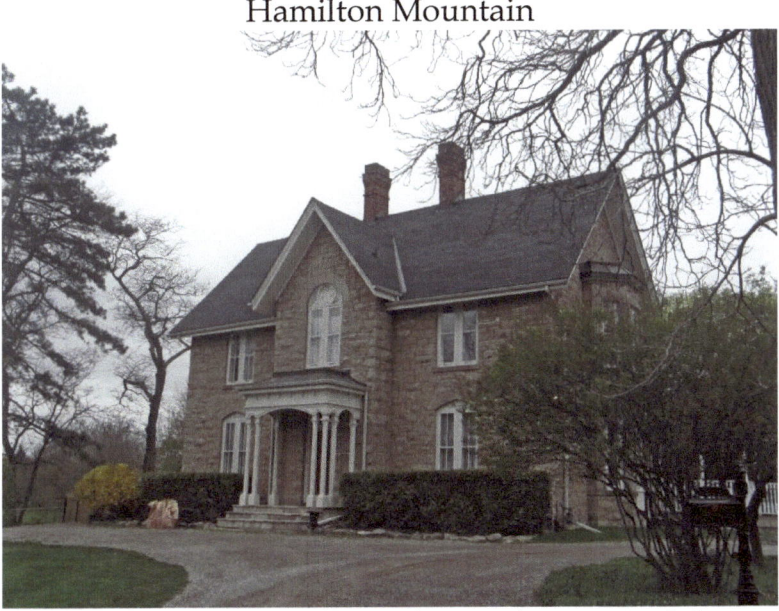

On Hamilton Mountain off Garth – Gothic Revival, limestone

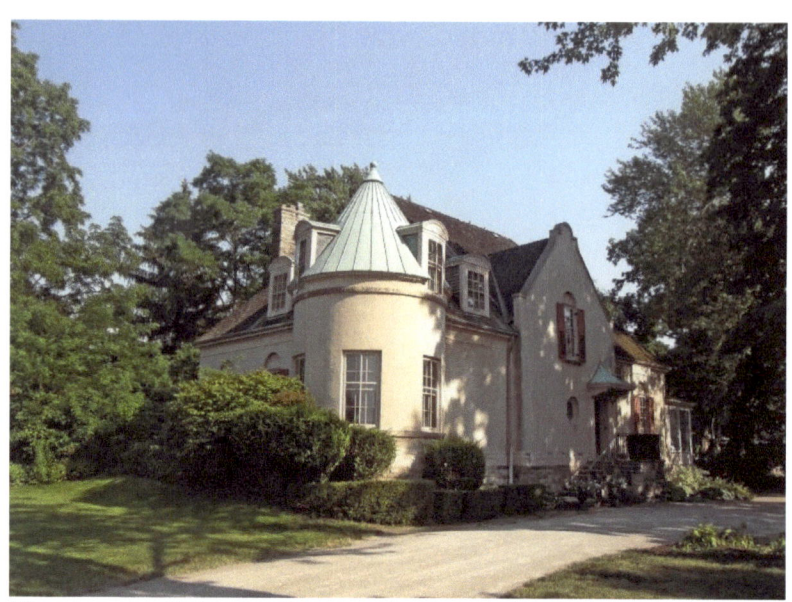

63 Claremont Drive – Queen Anne style chateau – built 1890, turret, dormers

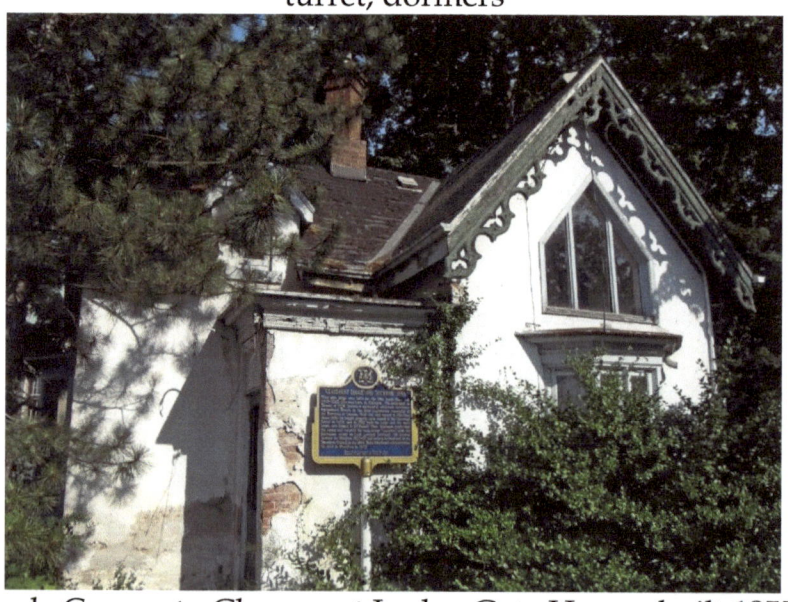

Arcade Crescent - Claremont Lodge Gate House, built 1855 as part of the Claremont Estate, Gothic Revival style, built for the Honourable Isaac Buchanan; verge board trim on gable

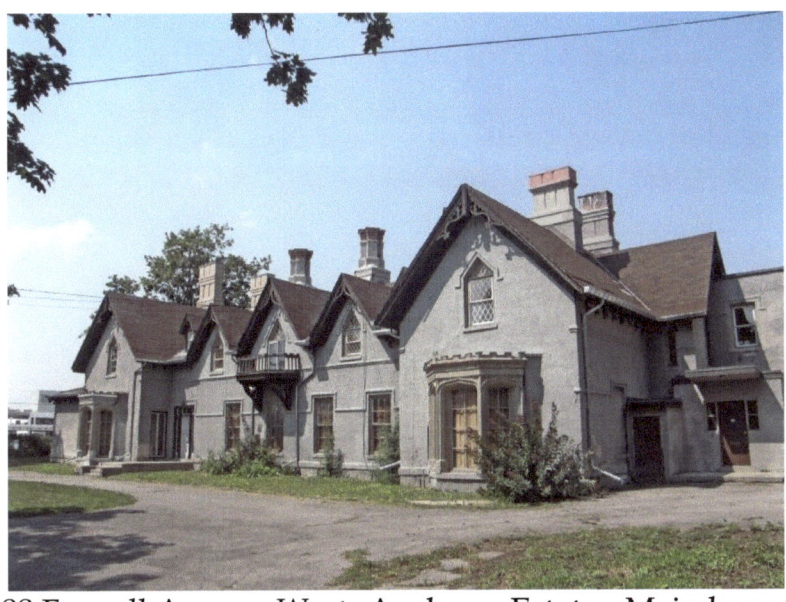

88 Fennell Avenue West -Auchmar Estate - Main house named after the Buchanan estate on Loch Lomond, Scotland, built 1852-1854 in the Gothic Revival style

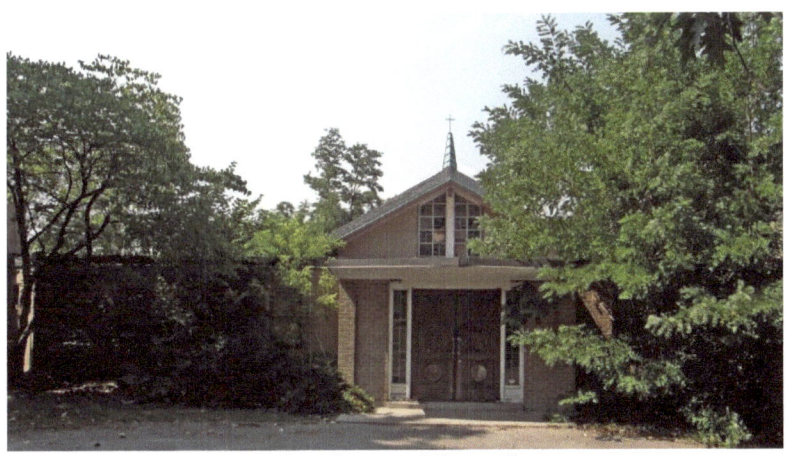

Auchmar Chapel

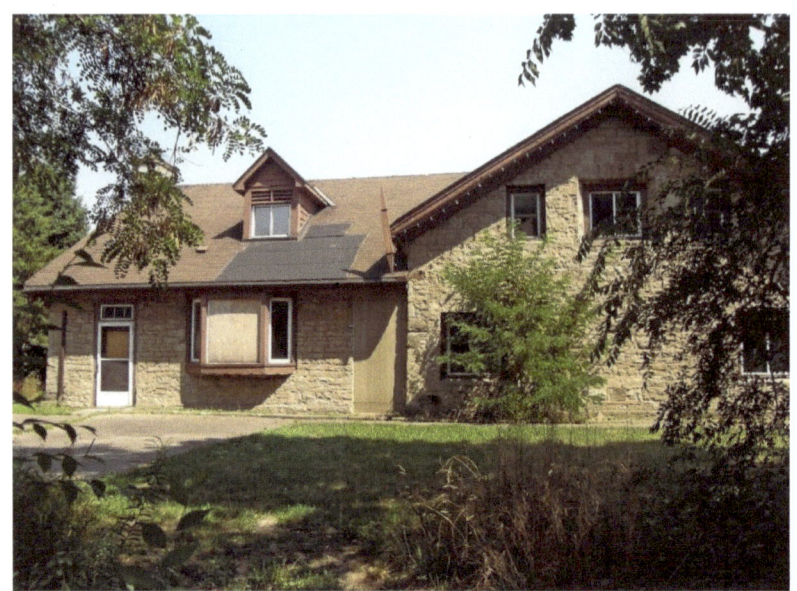

Building on Auchmar Estate

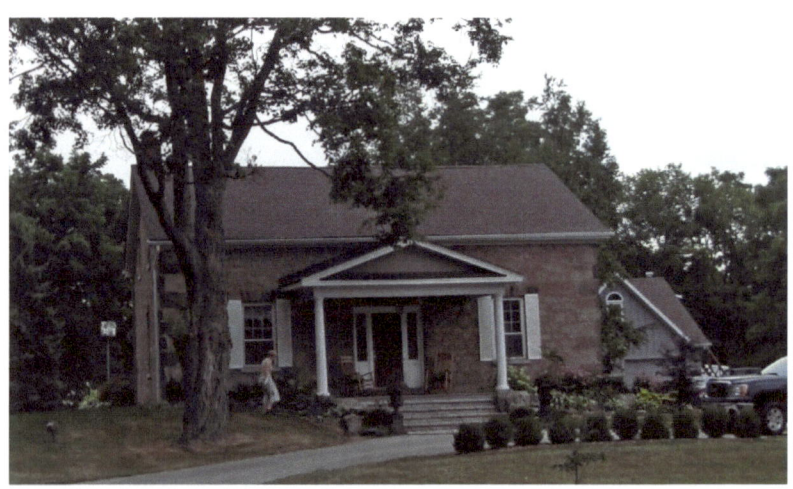

Highway 53 – pediment above porch

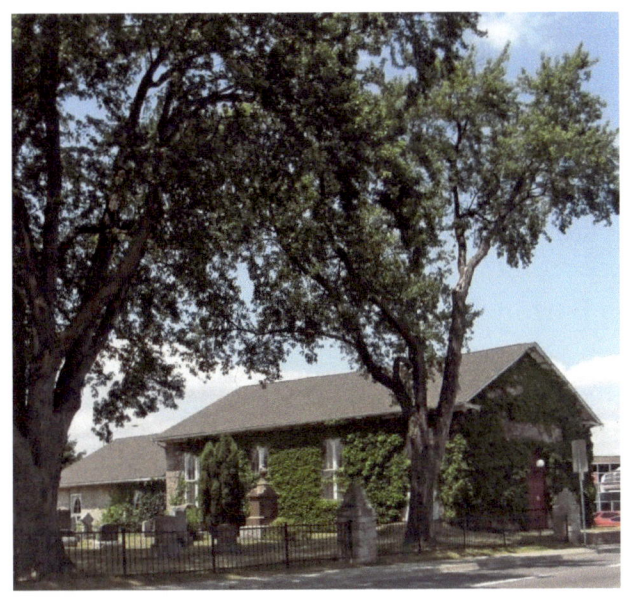

Barton Stone Church United, 21 Stone Church Road West
Built between 1845 and 1847

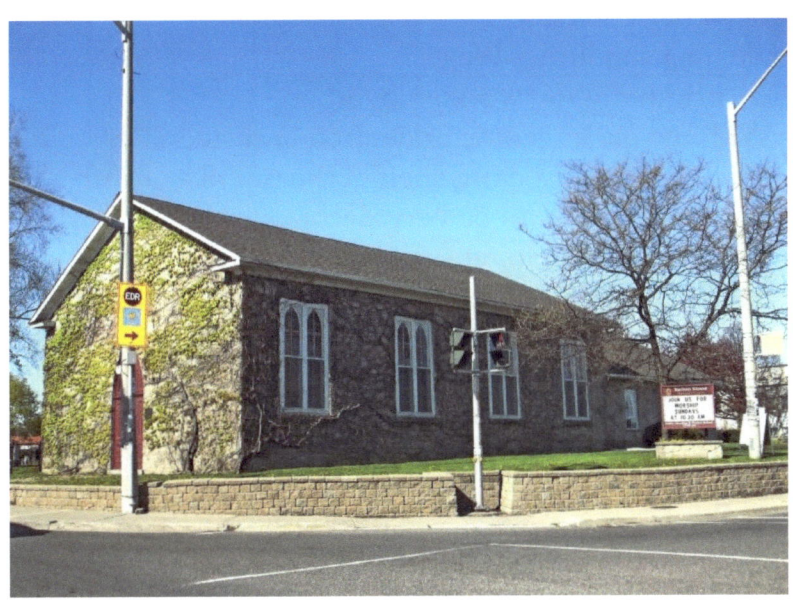

Architectural Terms

Brackets: a decorative or weight-bearing structural element which forms a right angle with one side against a wall and the other under a projecting surface such as an eave or roof. Example: 55 Barton Street West	
Buttress: a masonry structure built against or projecting from a wall which serves to support or reinforce the wall. In Canadian architecture, they are sometimes used for decoration. Example: Basilica of Christ the King	
Capital: The uppermost finish or decoration on a column. An Ionic column has a small base, a thin elegant shaft, and a capital composed of volutes which are carved whirls or twists that take the form of a scroll. Example: Jackson Street West	
Cornice: originally the wooden overhang of the roof. With the use of stone, brick, iron and steel, the cornice is any projecting shelf at the top of a ceiling or roof. They can be very decorative. Example: 141 George Street	
Cupola: A domed or curved roof rising from a building as a decorative element. Example: James Street North	
Dentil Moulding: an even series of rectangles used as ornamental decoration in cornices. Example: 55 Main Street West	

Dichromatic brickwork: the use of two colours of brick, tile or slate to decorate a façade. Example: 119-121 Jackson Street West	
Dormer: (French for "sleep") a gable end window that pierces through the plane of a sloping roof surface to create usable space in the top floor or attic of a building by adding headroom. Example: 22 Wesanford Place	
Gable: the triangular portion of a wall between the edges of a sloping roof. Example: 107 George Street	
Iron Cresting: A decorative ornament along the top of a roof. Iron cresting was popular in the Baroque era and also in Italianate, Victorian, Second Empire and Queen Anne styles of architecture. Example: Jackson Street West	
Mansard Roof: This style was popularized by Francois Mansart (1598-1666), an accomplished architect of the French Baroque period and especially fashionable during the Second French Empire (1852-1870). This roof is almost flat on the top section, with two slopes on each of its sides with the lower slope at a steeper angle than the upper and having dormer windows. Example: Jackson Street West	

Palladian Window: a large window that is divided into three sections with the centre section larger than the two side sections and usually arched. Example: Charlton Avenue (see Page 16)	
Pediment: a triangular section above the horizontal structure (entablature), typically supported by columns. The inside of the triangle is called the tympanum. Example: 360 James Street North	
Quoin: masonry blocks at the corner of a wall, often a decorative feature, usually larger or of a different colour than the rest of the wall. Example: 163 Jackson Street West	
Rose Window: a circular window with ornamental tracery radiating from the centre. Example: 21 Barton Street West	
Turret: a small tower that projects from the wall of a building. Example: 63 Claremont Drive	

Vergeboard and Finial: also called bargeboards – hang from the projecting end of a roof and are often elaborately carved and ornamented. **Finial:** ornament added to the top of a gable, pinnacle, canopy or spire – a Gothic element. Example: 123 Jackson Street West	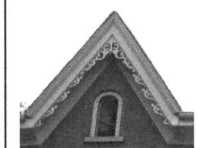
Window Hood: A **hood** is the piece found above window openings, usually of an ornate design, and covers the top third of the opening. Hoods are commonly placed above arched or curved openings on both windows and doors. Example: 163 Jackson Street West	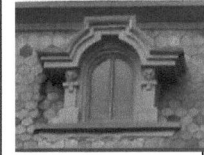

Building Styles

Art Deco, 1910-1940 - The Art Deco Style was developed for the French luxury market after World War I. Art Deco left its mark on everything from lamps and foot stools to purses and hair combs. The style was adopted in Ontario by wealthy and very fashionable patrons who wanted Art Deco detailing to make their buildings look lavish and exotic. Example: Go Station (see Page 28)	
Beaux Arts: Promoters of this style sought to express the classical principles on a grand and imposing scale. Many of the Beaux Arts buildings were banks, post offices, and railway stations. The Ontario Beaux Arts style is eclectic mixing elements of Classical, Renaissance and Baroque. Often the designs have a temple-like façade, pedimented porticos, balustrades, capitals in many styles. Example: 55 Main Street West	
Classical Revival (1820 - 1860) – This style was an analytical, scientific, and dogmatic revival based on intensive studies of Greek and Roman buildings, concerned with the application of Greek plans and proportions to civic buildings. Schools, libraries, government offices, and most other civic buildings were built in the Classical Revival style. The white columned porches of the Classical Revival domestic buildings are identified with the mansions of wealthy land owners in Canada. Example: 47 James Street South	

Edwardian, 1900-1930 – This style bridges the ornate and elaborate styles of the Victorian era and the simplified styles of the 20th century. Balanced facades, simple roof lines, dormer windows, large front porches, and smooth brick surfaces are its characteristics. Example: see Page 16	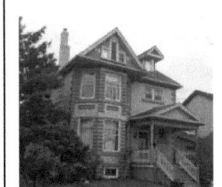
Gothic Revival, 1830-1890 – These decorative buildings have sharply-pitched gables with highly detailed vergeboards, pointed-arch window openings, and dichromatic brickwork. It is a common style in Ontario. Example: 123 Jackson Street West	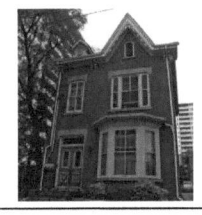
Italianate, 1850-1900 – It has wide-bracketed eaves, belvederes, wrap-around verandahs. Example: 153 George Street	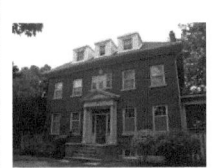
Neo-Classical (1810 - 1850) – This style was a direct result of the War of 1812. Many Upper Canadians returning from the war with the United States were second or third generation Loyalists who had inherited land and means from their forefathers. Once the conflict had passed, they had the money and the time to expand their holdings and indulge their architectural whims. Both residential and commercial buildings were constructed on the traditional Georgian plan, but they had a new gaiety and light-heartedness. Detailing became more refined, delicate, and elegant. Example: 1-5 Main Street West	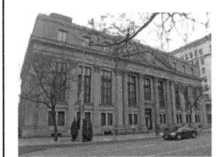

Queen Anne, 1885-1900 – This style is distinguished by an irregular outline featuring a combination of an offset tower, broad gables, projecting two-storey bays, verandahs, multi-sloped roofs, and tall, decorative chimneys. A mixture of brick and wood is common. Windows often have one large single-paned bottom sash and small panes in the upper sash. Example: 63 Claremont Drive	
Romanesque Revival, 1880-1910 – This style hearkens back to medieval architecture of the 11th and 12th centuries with a heavy appearance, blocky towers and rounded arches. Example: 24 Main Street West	
Second Empire, 1860-1880 – The mansard roof is the most noteworthy feature of this style and is evidence of the French origins. Projecting central towers and one or two-storey bays can also be present. Example: Jackson Street West (see Page 41)	

www.ingramcontent.com/pod-product-compliance
Lightning Source LLC
Chambersburg PA
CBHW040840180526
45159CB00001B/254